Why Black Lives Do Matter

Why Black Lives Do Matter
by
Earl Ofari Hutchinson

MID|DLE
PASS|AGE
PRESS

Huck: "We Blowed out a cylinder head."
Aunt Sally: "Good gracious! Anbody hurt?"
Huck: "No'm; killed a nigger."
Aunt Sally: "Well, it's lucky; because sometimes people
            do get hurt."

—An exchange in Mark Twain's *Huckleberry Finn*

Why Black Lives Do Matter

Copyright © 2018 Earl Ofari Hutchinson
All rights reserved including the right of reproduction in whole or in part in
any form.

Printed in the United States

Published by
Middle Passage Press
5517 Secrest Drive
Los Angeles, California 90043

Indexed by Barbara Bramwell Hutchinson
Designed by Alan Bell

Publisher's Cataloging-In-Publication Data
(Prepared by The Donohue Group, Inc.)
Names: Hutchinson, Earl Ofari.
Title: Why black lives do matter / by Earl Ofari Hutchinson.
Description: [Los Angeles, California] : Middle Passage Press, [2018] |
Includes bibliographical references and index.
Identifiers: ISBN 9781881032038
Subjects: LCSH: African Americans—Social conditions—21st century. |
Racism—United States. | United States—Race relations. | Racial profiling in
law enforcement—United States. | African Americans—Civil rights. | Black
lives matter movement.
Classification: LCC E185.615 .H88 2018 | DDC 305.8/00973—dc23

Library of Congress Control Number:
Middle Passage Press, Los Angeles, California

Table of Contents

Why Black Lives Do Matter

Introduction

In spring 2017, Trump met with the Congressional Black Caucus. The issue was welfare reform, and how his version of it would have a detrimental impact on welfare recipients. Many of whom, it was noted, weren't Black. A non-ruffled Trump quickly retorted, "Really? Then what are they?" The fact that the overwhelming majority of welfare recipients, are, and have always been, white likely didn't mean much to Trump. He was simply stating the popular belief that African-Americans are chronically, poor, downtrodden, and perennial government wards. The myth of the welfare queen raking in thousands of welfare dollars was fanned by President Ronald Reagan in the 1980s and quickly became a staple in the media's depiction of welfare recipients.

Five years earlier, *NBC News* anchor Brian Williams fed another popular stereotype about Blacks when he likely blatantly lied about being terrorized by gangs in New Orleans during the Hurricane Katrina debacle in 2005. Williams repeatedly said that during his stay at the Ritz Carlton Hotel in New Orleans covering the Katrina nightmare he and other guests and refugees at the hotel were assailed, assaulted, and threatened by an armed gang. Williams, as with his other dubious personal news coverage claims, got away with this whopper for years.

Williams' claim was unquestioned for two reasons. One was obvious. It was Williams saying it, and after all, would the respected face of American TV journalism, lie? The other reason was less obvious, but far more insidious. The assumption was that the gangs were young Black males, since the media early on latched on to the narrative that New Orleans before, during, and in the immediate aftermath of Katrina was being held siege by desperate, criminal bands of out of control Black thugs. Despite all evidence to the contrary that debunked this lie, it was looped so long and so often it became accepted fact.

The welfare cheat and the inherently crime prone young Black males standard depiction are just two of the storehouse of racial stereotypes that remain a staple of ingrained negative depictions of Blacks. They have had deadly consequences for Blacks, from police killings to disparities in education, health care, housing, employment, and the impoverishment of millions of Blacks.

There was another development that offered a stark counter to this. In April 2018, a near tearful Starbucks CEO Kevin Johnson told millions in a series of major network TV interviews that he was deeply hurt and found "reprehensible" the action at one of the company's more than 8000 Starbucks. The action was the arrest of two Black men at a Starbucks in Philadelphia. The men were arrested after the manager called the police under the pretense that they were loitering and refused to leave. The arrest was captured on tape and went viral. It ignited mass protests, denunciations of Starbucks by civil rights leaders and Black activists and many in the press. It was a PR disaster.

So, Johnson's heartfelt admission of the problem was more than standard PR fluff, and a media charm tour. He did swift damage control by vowing to make radical changes in employee training, community outreach, and more funding for minority community projects. He capped that with a meeting with, and a public apology, to the two men, and the announcement to close all Starbucks nationwide for a day for ramped up diversity training. It was big, sweeping and unprecedented corporate reaction to blatant racial profiling of the Black men. It was more. It was almost certainly the first time in American history that a major corporation shut down almost its entire operation for a day, at the cost of tens of millions in revenue, in response to blatant racism. This was the long-awaited template for how to decisively confront racism and the racist stereotypes that damage so many.

It was a huge step forward from the duck, dodge, and denial of the poison of racial stereotypes by many corporations and other business and public entities nearly a quarter century earlier when I wrote *The Assassination of the Black Male Image*, published in 1995. This is what I wrote then.

'He was 'dangerous,' of 'massive size,' 'threatening,' and 'a poor role model.' These were the words that several of the white jurors in the trial in 1992 of the four LAPD officers charged with beating Black motorist Rodney King described him to interviewers after the trial. I turned back the pages of history a century or more, and these were almost the identical words that Southern slaveholder apologist, Charles Carroll, pilloried blacks with in his grotesque little book published in 1900, *The Negro a Beast or in the Image of God.* Carroll was dead serious in making the case that blacks were left out of human creation and was a subspecies of the animal world. He sent years, he claimed, digging in the archives and consulting with theologians, academics, and scientists to prove his theory about inherent black primitiveness."

"Carroll didn't stop there with "science" to make his case against Blacks. He also retreated into Scripture. He swore that God warned that since creation the world's troubles had begun when human beings let the Negro 'beast' mingle among them. His book was not published by the Klan in rural Mississippi or Alabama, but by the American Book and Bible House in St, Louis. It was a brisk seller at the time and widely cited and quoted by many in academic circles. Reading the book without the filter of America's hideous racial past one might have reason to laugh today. But the stereotypes that Carroll propagated as scientific facts have had a powerful and enduring life of their own in the century plus since the book was published."

Nearly a quarter century after I wrote that a fierce battle

was still being waged to combat the negative stereotypes and typecasting of Blacks that continued to permeate much of the public's thought and actions toward African-Americans. This was not hyperbole. A poll taken by Reuters and Ipsos with the University of Virginia Center for Politics after the violent rampage by white nationalist groups in Charlottesville, Virginia in August 2017, found that nearly one out of three whites said they strongly or somewhat agreed that the country needs to "protect and preserve its White European heritage." Almost 30 percent said they neither agreed nor disagreed. Equally disturbing, nearly a third of respondents failed to express support of interracial marriage—with 16 percent agreeing outright that "marriage should only be allowed between two people of the same race."

* * * * *

The hope was that former President Obama's election in 2008 had buried once and for all negative racial typecasting and the perennial threat racial stereotypes posed to the safety and well-being of Blacks. It did no such thing. Immediately after Obama's election teams of researchers from several major universities found that many of the old stereotypes about poverty and crime and Blacks remained just as frozen in time. The study found that much of the public still perceived those most likely to commit crimes were poor, jobless, and Black. The study did more than affirm that race, poverty and crime were firmly rammed together in the public mind. It also showed that once the stereotype is planted, it's virtually impossible to root out. That was hardly new either.

In 2003, Penn State University researchers conducted a landmark study on the tie between crime and public perceptions of who is most likely to commit crime. The study found that many whites are likely to associate pictures of Blacks with violent crime. This was no surprise given the relentless media depictions of young Blacks as dysfunctional, dope-peddling, gang bangers, and drive-by shooters. The Penn State study found that even when Blacks didn't commit a specific crime; whites still misidentified the perpetrator as an African-American.

Eight years later, university researchers wanted to see if that stereotype still held sway, even as white voters were near unanimous that race made no difference in whether they would or did vote for Obama. Researchers still found public attitudes on crime and race unchanged. The majority of whites still overwhelmingly fingered Blacks as the most likely to commit crimes, even when they didn't commit them. Countless other studies have mirrored in one form or another the study's findings about the tightly held negative racial perceptions of African-Americans many Americans cling to.

The bulging numbers of Blacks in America's jails and prisons, the deadly encounters with police in which young Black males almost always unarmed are gunned down by police, seem to reinforce the wrong-headed perception that crime and violence in America invariably comes with a young, Black male face. There are innumerable counters, though, to the stereotypical typecasting of Blacks. They include the thousands of Black high achieving scholarship winners at major colleges and universities, the countless numbers of successful businesspersons, professionals and educators, and individuals such as James Shaw, Jr. who thwarted a mass killer at the Waffle House restaurant in Tennessee in April 2018. Shaw doubled-down on his sterling heroism by raising tens of thousands for the victim's families.

In my earlier work, *The Assassination of the Black Male Image* I took a laser look at the history of and continuing propagatio, of gross racial typecasting and stereotypes that make African-Americans the perennial target of racial and police violence. *Why Black Lives Do Matter,* is sweeping in scope and as laser in focus, and hits harder on the same devastating racial stereotypes of Blacks that I examined almost a quarter century earlier. It again assesses how racial typecasting continues to fuel the widespread public belief that Blacks are victimizers and not victims. This has stifled public debate and enabled political inaction, if not outright resistance, to meaningful solutions to the problem of racial victimization in American society. I detail a series of steps that have been taken by many groups and individuals in schools, business and public agencies to combat racial typecasting. I add to that more steps that can be taken to confront the problem.

I owe a debt of gratitude to the young men and women who formed Black Lives Matter that rammed the issue of police violence and its bedrock in racial stereotypes and fears on the nation's table. The devaluation of Black lives has truly been a chronic, painful, and all consuming American dilemma that screams for an end. In a small way, *Why Black Lives Do Matter* attempts to further that aim.

CHAPTER 1

Out of their League:
The Kaepernick Game Changer

He is "an athlete who is now widely recognized for his activism because of his refusal to ignore or accept racial discrimination." This had to be a strange declaration for Amnesty International Secretary General Salil Shetty to make about former San Francisco 49er Quarterback Colin Kaepernick. Why? Because it was the rarest of rare times that a professional athlete has been praised, let alone, honored by an organization such as Amnesty International (AI) for battling for human rights. AI is the one organization best known for its long-time, global dogged fight against human rights abuses, mostly by such tyrannical regimes as North Korea, Iran, the Congo, and a handful of other of the world's most notorious despotic rights abusers.

Yet, there was Kaepernick beaming on the podium in

Amsterdam, the Netherlands, in April 2018 receiving AI's Ambassador of Conscience Award. In his acceptance speech, Kaepernick was unapologetic in telling why he was standing on the podium and receiving the award, "Racialized oppression and dehumanization is woven into the very fabric of our nation—the effects of which can be seen in the lawful lynching of black and brown people by the police, and the mass incarceration of black and brown lives in the prison industrial complex ." "Lawful lynching," "mass incarceration," the "prison industrial complex," these were terms that were almost unheard of uttered by a professional athlete, let along actually publicly fighting against these maladies in the sports world. That's a world that shells out tens of millions to Black athletes yearly. The unspoken price for the financial goodies they receive from pro teams is that they say and do nothing about racial issues.

By the time Kaepernick took the podium at the Amnesty International awards event, his stance against the triple ills he mentioned, and the blowback he received, were well known. That was his National Anthem kneel-down, the outspoken attack on the police murders of unarmed blacks, the furious assault by Trump, and many NFL owners against him, the protest in support of his action by many Black NFL players, and his subsequent blackballing from the NFL. He paid a steep price for speaking out. This included the loss of millions in salary and bonuses, the kiss off of lucrative commercial endorsements, and finally, his prolonged, and contentious lawsuit against the NFL. What was less discussed, and in some ways equally, if not more important, in the Kaepernick drama was what he did off-the field, beyond speaking out against racial injustice and police violence. He assigned to himself the quiet role as mentor, philanthropist, and motivator to youth education and social justice organizations. That was a major game changer. Kap, however, did more than put his money and mouth where his heart was. He took the kind of action that could and should serve as a model for other pro athletes who have major name recognition, star power, fan and media acclaim, and the resources to really make a difference in the lives of at risk Black males and females.

* * * * *

The first public inkling that Kaepernick was on a mission to engage with young Blacks came in October 2017. Kap talked candidly to students at DREAM Charter School in Harlem. It wasn't so much his words to the students about the importance of activism in their community. It was that he was there at all. This was the time of the year that he, as every other NFL player, would be preparing for the 3rd or 4th game of the 2017 NFL season. Though he was out of the NFL, he didn't have to be at a Harlem school that month. But he was. His presence there sent the powerful message that dealing with life's problems and struggles in inner city neighborhoods was more important than chasing the fleeting glory of the gridiron. In the weeks after his talk at the Harlem school, Kap did more than just preach activism to the students, he made substantial donations to a range of other youth education and social justice organizations and programs.

He made his new-found role as committed philanthropist official when he announced in November 2017 that he had launched "the Million Dollar Pledge" campaign through his foundation. He'd give his money and challenge other athletes and donors to give their money to bankroll a number of community groups working in the area of education and criminal justice reform. The challenge to other athletes and celebrities was especially important. This was a way that they could give to self-help community organizations without fearing they'd take for being involved in controversial issues. Much of the money donated went to organizations that provided support for programs such as a homeless shelter for women. That could hardly be considered politically threatening. Yet to the women in need of those services it was manna from heaven.

More important than their dollars, was that they showed those in poor, underserved communities that there are Black celebrities and athletes who do not fit the media fostered stereotype of the self-indulgent, often reckless, irresponsible, Black athlete. That was depicted as only concerned with the flash, the glitter, and living the high life. And when their playing days were over, they often found themselves dead-broke, practically pushing a shopping cart on the streets. The other negative image of these athletes was that of someone who has risen out of impoverished conditions, but ignored, or worse scoffed at those who weren't blessed with superb athletic skills.

These stereotypical images of Black athletes that have

been drilled home in the mind of much of the public have had disastrous consequences for these athletes. A 2015 University of Missouri School of Journalism study found that news outlets were far more likely to print or headline stories about Black athletes busted for criminal acts, domestic violence, or drug use than for white athletes. It takes no imagination to see that if the Black athlete is depicted as crime prone, and violent Athlete, their celebrity or athletic status will not shield them from the myriad insults, digs, and dangers other Black males face.

*　*　*　*　*

The truth, though, is that Kaepernick was hardly the first Black celebrated athlete to smash these stereotypes of Black athletes and to provide positive modeling and support in poor Black communities. Magic Johnson, Lebron James, Chris Paul, Tiger Woods, Russell Wilson, and Serena Williams to name just a few have been outspoken in defying the negative athlete typecast and giving back to Black communities. They were not the exception. Many others openly and quietly established foundations, charities, scholarship programs, sports camps, and business entities that provided funding for an array of programs for inner city Black youth. A few years ago, one Black news outlet detailed just what types of programs and causes star Black athletes gave to.

- NBA star Dwight Howard—Funded programs to provide school supplies, clothes, and toys to Haitian school children.

- NBA Former star Dikembe Mutombo-Funded programs to eradicate childhood diseases in the Congo.
- Former NFL star Tony Gonzalez-Funded programs to assist medically challenged children tackle physical abilities or limitations as well as support for Boys and Girls Clubs that target at risk youth for assistance.
- New York Yankees all-star outfielder Curtis Granderson-Established a program to provide educational resources and assistance to schools nationwide as well as re-establishing baseball opportunities for inner city youths.
- Magic Johnson's on-going fund raising for community-based organizations sports, education, health, job and skills training, financial literacy, and business development training in ethnically diverse, urban communities throughout the nation.

These are programs and causes that they felt passionate about and were willing to use their name and fame to inspire young persons to achieve. There were also organizations such as United Athletes Foundation, which was established in 2008 to provide an avenue for athletes to donate to various causes in communities. At the time it was formed, it listed 90 professional athletes from the NBA, WNBA, NFL, MLB and professional boxing committed to its donor program. The number of athletes involved in the foundation has markedly grown since then.

* * * * *

There's really nothing new about the willingness of

prominent Black Athletes to do more than chase money, fame and glory, win bushels of awards and championships, and live the life of the rich and famous. Muhammad Ali sacrificed the prime years of his athletic life, faced imprisonment for his stance against racial injustice. That history is well known and remembered. But much less known and remembered is that many of the top Black athletes beginning in the late 1960s played big roles in establishing and funding programs, projects and mentoring at risk Black youth.

Tennis star Arthur Ashe typified the elevated racial awareness of many Black Athletes. When asked if his battle with HIV/AIDS was the hardest thing he had to deal with, he famously said, " No, the hardest thing I've ever had to deal with is being a Black man in this society." His outspoken crusade against South African apartheid and the treatment of Haitian refugees in the 1970s, including an arrest for protesting their treatment during a demonstration at the White House in 1992, got a lot of ink. But Ashe also was a tireless advocate for academic excellence for Black athletes, while raising millions for inner-city tennis centers and the United Negro College Fund.

Decades before Ashe and Kap, baseball great Jackie Robinson set the template for defying the stereotype of the all brawn and no brain, and devil may care Black athlete This has nothing to do with Robinson's breaking the color barrier in Major League Baseball in 1947. It had everything to do with what Robinson did off the field. He was a major fund raiser and speaker for Dr. Martin Luther King's Southern Christian

Leadership Conference in the 1960s, marched in numerous civil rights demonstrations, and funded education programs, mentored youth, and employed countless numbers of young Blacks in Harlem in restaurants that he represented. Robinson understood the score on racial injustice and the need to fight it. He made it clear that the Black athlete had a special role to play in that fight. He punctuated that with his famed quip, "I never had it made." In the late 1960s, NFL great, Jim, Brown, followed Robinson's example. He established the Black Economic Union. Brown's effort was not a lone effort. In a short time, many other Black athletes such as NBA superstar Bill Russell joined the organization. The explicit aim was to invest in and establish businesses and encourage self-help programs in inner city neighborhoods.

Later Brown reflected on the mission and success of the Union, "We were always interested in education, in history, we knew our history. We knew how to start businesses. [We] created the Black Economic Union in the '60s. [We] got over a million dollars from the Ford Foundation. [We] had a national business planning team. [We] had athletes and MBAs combined. The MBAs with their knowledge and the athletes with their promotional ability and the money. [We] started over 400 black businesses." Brown didn't stop there, when James and other NBA players protested the police killing of Michael Brown in Ferguson, Missouri in 2014 and other unarmed Blacks, Brown applauded them for "intelligently protesting what they feel are injustices."

The past and present history of protest and the

willingness by Black Athletes to shatter racial stereotypes and engage with Black communities has been a great boon for the players and for many youth in impoverished Black communities. This was great for Kap too in that he could claim much of the credit for shaking up the NFL and the sports world, much of the sports establishment, and even causing a significant number of NFL and sports fans to think hard about police abuse and racial injustice in society.

Ironically, this is where he, and the many that rallied to his side, and who saw him as a living, breathing model to inspire achievement in young Blacks, while smashing the stereotype of the dumb, socially clueless Black athlete, lost and gained. The loss was that he and others would continue to be vilified, scorned, and ridiculed by many in the sports establishment and other NFL fans and sports enthusiasts as the ones who ruined football and sports by ramming those inconvenient issues and politics into the sports arena. Kap would be the Curt Flood of pro football; a man who took a stand, won a victory for the players, but who paid a heavy personal price for that victory.

It's facile to say that he had any desire to be the Rosa Parks of sports. He was a pro football player, first and foremost. That's what he would have almost certainly have loved to continue to be. That was not to be. However, in the end his personal loss was Black America's gain.

This was crucial in that it served as one more much needed counter to the hideous history of America's racial typecasting of Blacks. That history is still very much evident in the way Blacks are seen both on and especially off America's playing fields. Therefore, this history must constantly be re-examined, understood, and fought against.

CHAPTER 2

Toms, Coons, Mammies, and The Confederacy: Now and Forever

The tag on the couch may have been a silly mistake, but there was no mistake that swapping, selling and collecting the huge array of racist furnishings and home decorative pieces is a brisk and lucrative business. These items adorn thousands of American homes. There was a Coon Chicken Inn dinner plate, and a little Black Sambo Block. They sold for hundreds of dollars. An original Aunt Jemima Cookie Jar could net upwards of $2000. There are hundreds of counterfeit jars on the market. They sell for only a few dollars. The original Jolly Nigger Bank made in the early 1900s sells for hundreds of dollars at auctions. The hundreds of fakes of this grotesque little item are sold at swap meets and on the Internet for a few dollars.

This is not a made-up story of vicious racist stereotype collectibles that were commonly found in shops, stores, and in many American homes prior to World War II. These are racist collectibles that were found in stores in 2017. For instance, the All Metals Products Company, an outfit out of Michigan, originally made the Sambo Dart Boar. In 1940. Fifty years later the AAA Sign Company, an Ohio company reproduced the item as a decorative tin sign and for a time mass marketed it for about $15 dollars. AAA Sign also made and sold hundreds of wall clocks, ashtrays, and plates that were emblazoned with choice depictions of Sambos, Mammies, Toms and Coons. There's more than one kitchen in America where the cook light ups their stove with matchboxes that have Nigger Head Shrimp, Nigger Head Oysters, and Mammy Brand Oranges on the box cover.

The sale in racist furnishings is so good that many other countries have jumped into the business. The fake Jolly N Banks, for instance, are made in Taiwan exclusively for the American market. Japan and Korea manufacturers have also churned out thousands of racially offensive products.

These items are more than just historical curiosity pieces. They are almost certainly the butt of jokes, scorn, ridicule, and are used to degrade African-Americans by many that sit, lie, or gaze at these items in private homes. But that's exactly what they were originally intended to do.

The sale of racist collectibles with no disclaimer, or warning, and with no attempt made to sensitize buyers and sellers to the historic damage these items still wreak on African-Americans is a tragic mix of commercial irresponsibility and racially tinged indifference.

It also reflects the dangerous and mistaken notion that racist collectibles that portray the tom, coon, and mammy image of Blacks merely reflect a by-gone era when Blacks were viciously and publicly racially mugged. A century ago, newspapers and magazines had great fun ridiculing, lampooning, butchering and assailing Blacks in articles and cartoons. They were branded as "lazy," "brutes," "savages," "imbeciles," and "moral degenerates." Plantation songs, tales, and slave caricatures were wildly popular up until World War II. The Uncle Remus "darky" character immortalized in Walt Disney's classic, *Song of the South,* was wildly popular on the screen, in tunes, and in stories then, and today as well.

Quaker Oats continued to peddle the bandanna wearing, fat, dark-skinned mammy image of Black womanhood on its pancake boxes until 1989. That era is far from past. Legions of college fraternities were nailed in the year since 2015 for holding slave auctions, minstrel shows, and displaying the Confederate flag in front of frat dorms, and for their members sporting the flag on tee shirts. A lengthening parade of politicians, sports figures, celebrities, and shock radio talk jocks have been called on the carpet for making racist wise cracks, jokes, tongue slips, and flat out slurs of African-Americans.

Museums, art houses, and private collectors, including many African-Americans, routinely buy, sell, and swap racist furnishings too. They use the racist pieces to educate the public about the terror of America's vile, and shameful racist past. They also act as a constant reminder that that past can rear its hideous head time and again. However, thousands of other Americans that plop their dollars down for racist furnishings, as well as the manufacturers of them, aren't interested in their historic value, or in making and using them to educate others on the danger of racial intolerance. They're interested in making a buck even if means demeaning Blacks.

* * * * *

However, as repulsive as it is in discovering the still widespread availability of these items in stores and shops, it's even more disconcerting to discover that tens of thousands of these vicious racist collectibles are even more widely available on-line. There's this descriptive teases for two items that for a time were for sale on eBay that called the collector's edition of *Ten Little Nigger Boys and Ten Little Nigger Girls,* a "really sweet little old book."

And it described a print titled "Nigger in the Woodpile" as "adorable."

There were also approving teases for Bob's Uncle Little Nigger Boy Card Game, "Nigger" antique glass sets, moneyboxes, tobacco tins and racially offensive music scores, as well as the dozens of other similar items for sale on eBay as late as 2003.

This rogues' gallery of racially grotesque items dates mostly from pre-World War II days when racial slander, slurs and vilification of African-Americans were standard fare in

America. There's nothing wrong with collectors privately selling and trading racially vile collectibles, to each other, to antique houses or to museums. But their sale on eBay, which boasts that it is the world's online auction site, blatantly violates that company's own policy statement to "disallow" any material that promotes racial hatred, violence or intolerance. There was no eBay disclaimer or warning that these items are racially damaging.

Their presence on eBay, and the lack of an explanation as to why these offensive items have been banned from display in many schools and libraries, is less a damning indictment of America's odious racial past than a revealing showcase of current attitudes. A reexamination of that past reveals why the old racial stereotypes embodied in the array of racist books and collectibles on eBay stubbornly defy extinction. The stereotypes were propagated in those pre-World War II days by some of the loftiest and most respected academic publication in America.

Popular Science Monthly, The Annals of the American Academy of Political and Social Science, Medicine and the *North American Review* and other leading magazines chimed in with volumes of heady research papers, articles and scholarly opinions that claimed Blacks were hopelessly inferior, crime and violence-prone defectives from which society had to be protected. A flood of racist, pseudo scholarly books purported to prove that Blacks were inherently dangerous and mentally deformed, and that whites had to be defended from them at all costs.

Films of that era such as "Rastus in Zululand," "Rastus and Chicken," "Pickaninnies" and "Watermelon and the Chicken" unabashedly visually mugged the Black image. Then there were the high-art classics, "Birth of a Nation," that slavishly glorified the Ku Klux Klan and "Gone With the Wind" that promoted the phony Old South notion of Blacks as eternally blissful, happy-go-lucky slaves. Both films are still shown regularly on Turner Movie Classics, at film festivals and in art houses, often with no explanation or discussion as to how they incited racial violence and perpetuated racial stereotypes.

With the passage of three civil rights bills in the 1960s, numerous affirmative action statutes, stacks of court decisions that guarantee civil rights and civil liberties protections and the spectacular rise of a prosperous and politically connected Black middle class, the assumption was that America's ugly racial past had permanently been exorcised. But even if eBay had not sold and advertised a mountain of racist books, prints and collectibles, the old racial notions of Black inferiority and menace have been sneakily recycled in other ways.

In the 1970s, a whole new vocabulary of covert racially loaded terms such as "law and order," "crime in the streets," "permissive society," "welfare cheats," "subculture of violence," "subculture of poverty," "culturally deprived" and "lack of family values" seeped into the language about Blacks. Some politicians seeking to exploit white racial fears routinely tossed about these terms. In the 1980s, terms such as "crime prone," "war zone," "gang infested," "crack plagued," "drug turfs," "drug zombies," "violence scarred," "ghetto outcasts" and "ghetto poverty syndrome" were introduced into public discourse. These were covert racial code phrases for Blacks, and further reinforced the negative racial images.

eBay ignored the pleas of many Black eBay customers to honor its pledge to "disallow" racially vile items. And the sellers of these items, who regard them as cute and adorable, apparently gave little thought that many find them repugnant. This guarantees that the old racial stereotypes will never die.

There was one bright spot, though, in the battle to confront the hurt that racial stereotypes have caused. That came with the April 2018 edition of *National Geographic* magazine. "We thought we should examine our own history before turning our reportorial gaze on others," said the magazine's editor-in-chief, Susan Goldberg. The "reportorial gaze" she referred too was the admission that the magazine through its long history had been one of the main offenders in either excluding Blacks or pandering to the standard vile stereotypes and representations of Blacks as little more than "savages" and "primitives" in their photo spread and stories on Africa and other places.

Still, the enduring racist depictions of Blacks weren't the only intransigent, ever present means to preserve the negative perceptions of Blacks in the belief systems of millions of Americans. There's also the thousands of institutions that proudly bear the name or the emblem of America's warped racial past. The most prominent still are on schools and public buildings.

* * * * *

In 2015, there were more than twenty-two elementary schools in Texas, Alabama, Mississippi, Virginia, Oklahoma, Arkansas, Missouri, as well as in Long Beach and San Diego, California that were named after the top Confederate general Robert E. Lee. The even bigger irony and insult is that a significant number of minority students attend some of these schools. The school in Long Beach, California, for instance, is in a city that's one of the most ethnically diverse cities in California. To have a school there named after one whose military prowess bolstered Southern slavery and Jim Crow should have been cause for embarrassment.

Lee's superb battlefield generalship kept the Confederacy in play for four long and bloody years. It also insured four more years of brutal bondage for millions of African-Americans and a century after that of vicious, ruthless, and unrelenting terror, murder, pillage, Apartheid like segregation, grinding poverty, and gaping racial disparities in health, education, and the criminal justice system for many Blacks. The South and the nation certainly can thank Lee for much of that.

The issue of erasing the name of the South's most infamous general from an elementary school couldn't be separated from the ongoing battle to scrap the Confederate flag from statehouses, the sale of the flag and other Confederacy related items from major retail outlets, and the continued glorification of the South's treasonous act of rebellion and defiance of the Constitution. The Confederate flag was always much more than a symbol of a dead, archaic, and disgraceful past in American history. It has been a rallying point for the conservative assault on affirmative action, voting rights protections, and the expansion of civil rights laws. It was no accident that the Confederate flag was proudly and defiantly waved at Tea Party marches, protests and rallies ripping former President Obama during the first two years of his administration.

It was also no accident that GOP political leaders for years maintained either a stony silence on the removal of the flag and other Confederate monuments from statehouses and other public places or openly backed their continued display

When the name of the South's most famed Confederate general is on a school it is more than simply recognition of and tribute to an individual who fought to uphold slavery. The bigger problem is that teachers and school administrators at such a school are duty bound to benevolently cite Lee as an American patriot and a man who represents the highest ideals of American history and values to generations of students at the school. There is generally little effort made to include in Lee's record the horrors of slavery and racial vilification of African-Americans.

School officials in the Deep South knew that slapping Lee's name on an elementary school did much more than just idolize their hero. It also guaranteed that future generations of students who attend a school named in honor of Lee would also honor him and the rose colored historical depiction of him. The South's tortured history of slavery, Jim Crow segregation, and conservative reaction against civil rights laws and protections would be brush stroked from their education about Lee and the South and the continuing devaluation of Black lives that go with that very real still present history.

*   *   *   *   *

This is not mere polite, parlor or academic musing about the past or a name on a school or public building. The history and the racial stereotypes that this reinforces invariably rear their head in ugly action in deadly ways. In June 2014, there was some surprise that in between U.C. Santa Barbara's mass murderer Elliot Rodger's warped, sick, and perverse harangues against women, he also laced in a generous dose of racist rage and stereotyping.

"I passed by this restaurant and I saw this Black guy chilling with 4 hot white girls. He didn't even look good. Then later on in the day I was shopping at Trader Joe's and saw an Indian guy with 2 above average White Girls!!!"

He returned to these hate mongering digs at Black, Hispanic and Asian-American men for having the temerity to associate with white women, and worse their reciprocation with minority men more than a few times.

Rodger's murderous psychosis was certainly evident in these rants. That didn't tell the whole story of why a conflicted mixed-race young guy would act out his rage in a deadly spree against innocents. The racial targeting can well be chalked up to ignorance, confusion, racial denial, and closet bigotry. But there were several compelling hints that the racial blinders were tied chokingly tight on many whites, particularly young whites, as well as those who are conflicted about race, such as Rodger.

Racial digs that mock Blacks have been a common feature on more than a few college campuses in recent times. There's the wave of fraternities that have been called on the carpet for mocking Black notables and rappers. Many have also been reprimanded for their vicious mocking of Latin and Asian immigrants. This was not merely a free speech issue, or a case of zany college kids making utter fools of each other. This was blatant racial slander.

An AP poll in 2012 found that a majority of non-Blacks had anti-Black prejudices. It also found that a significant number of those who held the same prejudices and outright bigoted views were in the under age 30 crowd. That's precisely the age demographic of Rodger. His rants proved once more that bigotry, with all its twisted, warped, and psychotic delusions, fears and hates could explode any time, and anywhere in the orgy of murderous rampages that Americans are getting far too accustomed to seeing and being victimized by. This never-ending jaded, highly colored by racial images and stereotypes of Blacks are tightly intertwined with racially charged violent actions and attacks. It's all made possible and easier when the attacker views the victim as a figure of totemic object of racial derision rather than a person. The enduring power of the old plantation images of the past are a testament to that.

The equally great testament to that is the memorabilia

that vilify Blacks rake in a lot of dollars for their sellers and traders. In other words their continued existence as hot commodities is a significant growth industry. It's more than race. It's a business.

CHAPTER 3

Buying into the Stereotypes

Comedian Bill Cosby was the walking, and then writing, proof of the ancient adage that good intentions can go terribly awry. That was never more painfully true than when his best-selling book *Come on People* hit the book stands in 2007. Cosby and his publisher boasted that the book was a big, brash, and provocative challenge to Black folk to get their act together. That got him rave raves and an unprecedented one-hour spin job on *Meet the Press*.

In the book, Cosby harangued and lectured, and cobbled together a mesh of his trademark anecdotes, homilies, and personal tales of woe and success. He juggled and massaged facts to bolster his self-designated Black morals crusade. Stripped away it was the same stock claim that Blacks can't read, write or speak coherent English, and are social and educational cripples and failures.

He succeeded marvelously in getting the tongues of Blacks wagging furiously and their fingers jabbing relentlessly at each other's alleged mountainous defects. Cosby's name was hopelessly disgraced by the mountain of allegations of rape, drugging, and sexual abuse, that resulted in countless lawsuits against him, the virtual whitewash of him from TV and the concert circuit, and two trials for sexual assault, and a 3 count felony conviction for sexual assault in a Pennsylvania court in April 2018. Yet, he was still vigorously defended by many Blacks. They stumbled over themselves to hail him as the ultimate truth-giver and claim that he was the victim of a racist conspiracy to bring down a wealthy, prominent Black man.

He wasn't. While Cosby was entitled to publicly air Black America's alleged dirty laundry, there was far more myth than dirt in that laundry. Some knuckleheads in Black neighborhoods do kill, mug, peddle dope, are jobless untouchables, and educational wastrels. They, and only they, should be the target of wrath. But Cosby made a Grand Canyon size leap from them to paint a half-truth, skewed, picture of the plight of poor Blacks and the reasons and prescriptions for their plight. The cornerstone of Cosby mythmaking was that they were crime prone, educational losers, and teen baby making machines.

The heart wrenching and much played up news shots and specials of black-on-black blood-letting in a handful of

big cities and the admission that Blacks do have a much higher kill rate than young whites for many was proof of out-of-
control, lawless Blacks. This is what Cosby railed against as
being somehow an inherent defect of Blacks. This rested on
myth. During the first decade and more of 2000, homicides
and physical assaults plunged among Black teens to the lowest
levels in decades.

The rate of drug use among young Blacks was never any
higher than among young whites. And countless surveys and
studies showed that Blacks are more likely to be arrested, convicted and imprisoned than young whites who if arrested at
all are more likely to get drug rehab, counseling, and treatment referrals, probation or community service. This all hor-
ribly distorted the racial crime picture. Then there is the Black
teen girls as baby making machine myth. The truth: The teen
pregnancy rate among Black girls also sharply dropped during the same time period.

The biggest myth that young Blacks empty out the public
schools, fill up the jails and cemeteries, and ridicule learning
as acting white has risen to urban legend rank. The truth:
The U.S. Dept. of Education found that in the decades since
1975, more blacks had enrolled in school, had improved their
SAT scores and had lowered their dropout rate significantly. It
also found that one in three Blacks attended college, and that
the number of blacks receiving bachelors and masters degrees
had nearly doubled. Surveys of student attitudes found that
Black students were as motivated, studied as hard, and were
as serious about graduating as whites.

Cosby publicly bristled at criticism that he took the worst of the worst behavior of some Blacks and publicly hurled that out as the warped standard of Black America. He claimed that he did not mean to slander all, or even most Blacks, as derelict, laggards and slackers. Yet that's precisely the impression he gave and the criticism of him for it was more than justified. Even his book's title, *Come on People: On the Path from Victims to Victors* (a hint they're all losers) conveyed that smear.

He never qualified or provided a complete factual context for his blanket indictment of poor Blacks. He made the negative behavior of some Blacks a racial rather than an endemic social problem. In doing so, he did more than break the alleged taboo against publicly airing racial dirty laundry; he fanned dangerous and destructive stereotypes.

That was hardly the call to action that could inspire and motivate underachieving Blacks to improve their lives. Instead, it further demoralized those poor Blacks who were doing their best to keep their children and themselves out of harm's way, often against towering odds, while still being hammered for their alleged failures by the Cosby's within and without their communities.

Worse, Cosby's blame the victim slam did nothing to encourage government officials and business leaders to provide greater resources and opportunities to aid those Blacks that need help. His book, the interviews and talks he gave on the subject during those years, were sold to many who wanted to believe the worst of the worst about Blacks as Gospel.

*   *   *   *   *

This was not the end of the Cosby engendered debate about warped racial images and typecasting of Blacks. In 2015, *Ebony* magazine stirred a mini-firestorm of rage when it dredged up an old photo shot of the TV Cosby show family, plopped it on its cover, and then fractured the picture. The obvious point being that the embattled comedian not only disgraced his legacy but disgraced the hitherto near sacrosanct image and legacy of the celebrated Cosby TV show family, the Huxtables. The premise of the show was that there was fully intact, respectable, high achieving, prim and proper Black middle-class families. The Huxtables was an in your face, counter to the ancient damaging, hurtful and false stereotype of the Black family and by extension Blacks, as crime, drug ridden, and dysfunctional, and eternally wallowing in ignorance and poverty single parent Black families.

The show's wild success and popularity was evidence that it gave many Blacks a positive, upbeat look at themselves, and the strengths of many Black families. It also gave many non-Blacks a glimpse of an upwardly mobile Black family that seemed to be no different than any other such family. The Ebony cover was under fire because it seemed to tear down the last remaining shred of what was good and decent about Cosby and the Black family.

The criticism badly ignored too much. Namely, that it was Cosby who in lectures, speeches, press appearances, and a best-selling book went on a one-man crusade to tell the world how supposedly lousy the Black family was.

Cosby's one sided, stereotypical laced crusade against alleged Black dysfunctionality was a zero sum catch 22 contradiction. If any of what Cosby said about the Black family's alleged chronic dysfunctionality was true, then that must mean that his be knighted Huxtable family was nothing more than a made for TV fraud. And that he and the show gamed millions to believe that such a Black family really existed, when it didn't. There were more than a few critics even then who knocked the Huxtables as just that, a myth, and lambasted the show and Cosby for creating the fairy tale image of an intact, achieving Black family. *Ebony's* fractured cover of the Huxtables merely messaged what Cosby had done long before his disgrace and fall; and that's publicly malign the Black family.

* * * * *

Cosby got much praise for his fan of racial stereotypes about Blacks. But he also got many hits for that. That was not the case for then Democratic presidential candidate Barack Obama when he thundered to long, loud and vigorous applause from a Father's Day Chicago church crowd in June 2008, that Black fathers don't engage with their children. A month before Obama made this stereotypical and plainly false assertion, Boston University professor Rebekah Levine Coley, in a comprehensive study on the Black family, found that Black fathers who aren't in the home are much more likely to sustain regular contact with their children than absentee white fathers, or for that matter, fathers of any other ethnic group.

The study was not an obscure study buried in the thick pages of a musty academic journal. It was widely cited in a feature article on Black fathers in the May 19, 2008 issue of Newsweek. There was no excuse then to spout this myth. The facts were totally contrary to Obama's knock.

Then again, this kind of over the top, sweeping talk about alleged Black father irresponsibility from Obama then wasn't new. In stump speeches, he pounded Black men for their alleged father dereliction, irresponsibility and negligence. Whether Obama was trying to shore up his family values credentials with conservatives or felt the need to vent personal anger from the pain and longing from being raised without a father was anybody's guess. (Note: his absentee father was not an African-American male but a Kenyan National who never intended to stay in this country). Or maybe he criticized Black men out of a genuine concern about the much media touted Black family breakup. Obama, though, clearly was fixated on the ever media popular notion of the absentee Black father. That fixation was fed by a mix of truth, half-truths and outright distortion.

Obama committed the cardinal error that every critic from the legions of sociologists, family experts, politicians and morals crusader Cosby who have hectored Black men for being father derelict have made. He omitted the words "some," "those," or "the offenders" before Black fathers. Instead, he made, or at least gave the impression, that all, or most, Black men aren't in the home, and are irresponsible. That being the case ipso facto they are the cause for the crime-drugs-violence-gross underachievement syndrome that young black males are supposedly eternally locked into.

Obama presented absolutely no evidence to back up this devastating indictment. The worse case estimate in 2015 was that slightly less than half of Black children live in fatherless homes. But that's only a paper figure. When income, education, individual background, and middle-class status are factored in the gap between Black and white children who live in intact two parent households is much narrower.

This points to the single greatest reason for the higher number of Black children who live in one parent households. That reason is poverty. Numerous studies have found that a Black father's ability to financially contribute the major support in the home is the major determinant of whether he remains in the home. That's no surprise considering that despite changing gender values and emphasis in society. The expectation and burden is still on men to be the principal breadwinner and financial provider. Put bluntly, men and the notion of manhood are still mainly defined by their ability to bring home the bacon. A man who falls short of that standard is considered a failure and loser.

The chronic near Great Depression levels of unemployment, not to mention rampant job discrimination, endemic failing public schools, and the stigma of a criminal record virtually condemn many young Black men to wear the tag of societal failures as men and fathers. Obama in his rap against Black men as fathers said nothing about the economic devastation that drives many Black men from the home or prevents them from being in the home in the first place.

Obama, undoubtedly was well intentioned in his criticism of Black family problems and certainly didn't mean to slander all, or even most Black men, as derelict, laggards and slackers as fathers. Obama, as Cosby and others who beat up on Black males for alleged father dereliction, would almost certainly publicly bristle at criticism that he took the worst behavior of some Black men and publicly hurled that out as the warped standard of Black America.

Yet that's precisely what was the inadvertent result. And since every utterance by him during his years in the White House was instant news it made his fan of stereotypes about Black men even more painful.

∗   ∗   ∗   ∗   ∗

Racial stereotypes whether propagated by presidents or celebrities, have had a rival in of all places the English language. No English language word has stirred more passion and outrage among Blacks than the word "n----r," or its politely sanitized version, the "N" word. In 1997 the offender was not a loose-lipped politician, celebrity, or athlete. It was none other than one of the bibles of the English language, *Merriam-Webster's Collegiate Dictionary.* The dictionary was the target of a national campaign by some black academics, local NAACP chapters, and *Emerge* magazine.

They claimed that Webster's redefinition of the word "n----r" racially stigmatized Blacks. They had a point. In the 1996 edition of *Webster's,* "n----r" was defined as "a Black person—usually taken to be offensive." It went even further and applied the word to "a socially disadvantaged person." It was easy to see the danger in *Webster's* redefinition. One could easily infer that the word "n---r" refers exclusively to blacks, the poor, and other nonwhites, and that all blacks are "socially disadvantaged." *Webster's* initially stuck to its guns and refused to bow to Blacks' complaints. *Webster's* editors insisted that that was the intent of the word. Then they went further. They justified the definition by claiming that Blacks use it among and about themselves, "Its use by and among Blacks is not always intended or taken as offensive." Apparently, this put the final stamp of racial approval on the word.

It was a self-serving point, but unfortunately, it was true. In issues of such popular Black magazines as *Essence* and *Emerge,* Black writers at times have gone through lengthy gyrations to justify using the word. Their rationale boiled down to this: The more a Black person uses the word the less offensive it becomes. They claimed that they are cleansing the word of its negative connotations so that racists can no longer use it to hurt Blacks. Comedian, turned activist, Dick Gregory, had the same idea when he titled his autobiography, "n----r." Black writer, Robert DeCoy, also tried to apply the same racial shock therapy to whites when he titled his novel, "The N---r Bible." Many Blacks say they used the word endearingly or affectionately. They say to each other, "You're my n----r if you don't get no bigger," or, "that N----r sure is something." Others use it in anger or disdain, "N----r you sure got an attitude," or, "A N----r ain't S---."

Still, other Blacks are defiant. They say they don't care what a white person calls them because words can't hurt them.

The Black defenders of the word have always missed the point. Words are not value neutral. They express concepts and ideas. Often words reflect society's standards. A word, as emotionally charged as "n---r," can reinforce and perpetuate stereotypes. The word "n----r" does precisely that. It is the most hurtful and enduring symbol of Black oppression. Novelist Richard Wright in his memorable essay, "The Ethic of Jim Crow," remembered the time he accepted a ride from a "friendly" white man. When the man offered him a drink of whiskey Wright politely said, "Oh, no." The man punched him hard in the face and said, "N----r ain't you learned to say, 'sir', to a white man?" The pain from the blow would pass, but the pain from the "N" word would stay with him forever.

During the era of legal segregation, some of America's major magazines and newspapers continued to treat Blacks as social outcasts. Historian Rayford Logan surveyed early issues of *Atlantic Monthly, Century Monthly, North American Review, Harpers, The Chicago Tribune, New York Times, The Boston Evening Transcripts, The Cincinnati Enquirer,* and *The Indianapolis Journal.* He noted that they routinely referred to blacks as "n————r," "niggah," "coon," and "darky." In news articles, Blacks were depicted as buffoons or dangerous criminals. The NAACP and Black newspaper editors waged vocal campaigns against racist stereotypes and the use of racist epithets. Black scholar, W.E.B. Dubois, frequently took white editors to task for refusing to spell "Negro" with an upper case "N." Dubois called their policy a "conscious insult" to Blacks. In that era, being called a Negro was a matter of pride and self-identity.

Even some of the Black defenders of the "N" word later realized their mistake and recanted. Following his return from a trip to Africa in the late 1970s, Richard Pryor told a concert audience that he would never use the word "n----r" again. The audience was stunned. The irreverent Pryor had practically made a career out of using the word in his routines. Pryor softly explained that the word was profane and disrespectful. He was dropping it because he had too much pride in Blacks and himself.

The election of Trump further fueled the climate of overt racial hostility and polarization. So, that made the use of the word even more fraught with danger. The public howl that it ignites when a white celebrity or politician sometimes slips and uses the word is commendable. However, equally commendable is the battle to get those African-Americans who use it to delete the word from their vocabulary as well. That battle dramatically underscores how the power of stereotypes, negative typecasting of Blacks has badly corroded even its victims.

CHAPTER 4

Bikers, Bombers, Terrorists and Racial Double Standards

By the summer of 2017, millions of Americans had seen it so often that it had become laughable, pitiable, and disgraceful. More than anything else it struck to the heart of a grotesque truth about American hypocrisy. The "it" this time was the blatant and outrageous casual, almost matter of fact, infuriating racial double standard by law enforcement, much of the press and public officials when it was young Black males committing mayhem versus young and not so young white males committing mayhem. There were the scenes of young whites overturning, defacing or torching cars, and buildings, and running wild in the streets blatantly defying police, with almost no fear of arrest or being clubbed, after a college or professional basketball or football team won a championship.

It's simply tagged as boys will be boys, acting out, and that's often even true in its worst form when a young white male shoots up a school or theater. What follows that is an endless string of psycho-babble pronouncements about his troubled childhood, drug and meds addiction, and dependence and psychological traumas. There were no indignant and furious calls from the press, citizenry, and elected officials for a swift, harsh, and massive crackdown, sweeps, and toss the book demands at them. The kind that is instantly heard when its young Blacks on the hot seat for committing a violent act.

Meanwhile, in 2015, the racial double-standard reared its ugly head again in the way that law enforcement handled and much of the media reported on the deadly shootout between two rival white Texas biker gangs in Waco. The carnage that left nine dead and scores wounded was, by any stretch, a public massacre. It was labeled a "feud," "a turf battle," accompanied by a deluge of interviews from self-identified biker gang members painting themselves as just another harmless, social club.

The violence was accompanied by a picture of scores of bikers who almost certainly in some way were connected with the mayhem, leisurely sitting on a roadside tweeting, surfing their cells, and chatting it up with each other. And just who nonchalantly sat beside them? Police officers seemingly just as casual; smiling, and in leisure as if it was just another day at the office. Or, as if they had just hauled these guys over and detained them for nothing more compelling than for a speeding violation.

＊　＊　＊　＊　＊

If the racial double standard in how white lawbreakers versus Black lawbreakers are depicted and treated is virtually a settled fact of public life, the even more dangerous double standard is when whites plant bomb that maim and murder dozens. When that happens, it ignites another debate why much of the media and with few exceptions law enforcement refuse to brand them domestic terrorists. The debate over that refusal was especially heated in the case of Mark Anthony Conditt, the Austin Bomber. If there was ever a case that the tag "terrorism" and the perpetrator labeled, "a terrorist" applied, it was the two-week reign of terror in March 2018 that Conditt traumatized Austin, Texas and other cities with. The facts sans Conditt's motive were clear.

He targeted and killed two African-Americans, and certainly more were on his kill list. He paralyzed a city. He stirred small army of FBI, ATF, and local police into action to hunt him down. He even got Trump to send a note of praise to law enforcement for finally bringing him to bay.

Yet, the words "terrorism" and "terrorist" were as usual nearly invisible from all official characterization of his made-in-America-terror rampage. Yes, some newspapers and commentators finally got it, and called him, and his acts, that. But there was no "official" branding of him and his actions as "terrorism" and "terrorist. The one official who was the most tight-lipped of all when it came to an absolute refusal to utter the two words "domestic" and "terrorist" when it came to mass murder by native born whites was Trump. He had plenty of opportunities since there were several major mass shootings and the Austin bombings on his presidential watch in 2017 and 2018. He passed every time the question was shouted at him to call these acts terrorist.

Instead, as usual, we got the by now standard playbook litany of half-baked veiled excuses and almost apologetics for his murderous deeds. The words and terms describing Conditt as "troubled," "a loner," 'hostile," and "no clue he was dangerous," from a good family" and now "anguished family" are standard for guys like him. The grand prize for media hand wringing about him went to one news outlet with this screaming headline, "An outcry from a challenged youth." "Outcry?" "challenged?" and a "youth?" Youth, he was 23 years-old, that's hardly comparable to a teen kid stealing hubcaps.

What made these veiled apologetics an even more disgusting example of an in your face dime store psychology attempt to deny domestic terrorism, was that almost within hours that he blew himself up, Sacramento police riddled Stephon Clark, an unarmed Black man with 20 bullets. Clark was one year younger than Conditt. Yet, there were none of the sympathetic pop descriptive analyses of Clark, let alone any in-depth picture of his family history and background.

Even more galling, according to FBI reports, between 2008 and 2012, about six percent of domestic terrorism suspects have been Muslim. The number of Blacks and Latinos that have committed domestic terror acts, be it mass shootings or bombings, has been almost negligible. In fact, the profile of a mass killer is that he's a he, a staunch gun nut, politically disgruntled, and a young white male. In a few cases, they were influenced by white supremacist groups.

The official fallback excuse of why the term isn't applied to white mass attackers is that there is no such charge—domestic terrorism—under federal law. That would entail acts "dangerous to human life and appear to be intended to intimidate or coerce a civilian population" or to influence government policy or conduct. This is not a criminal charge. In a Senate Hearing in September 2017, FBI Director Christopher Wray said as much, "There is not a domestic terrorism crime as such." There is no such hiding behind such scrupulous legalese when the perpetrator is a Muslim and a foreigner who plants bombs or shoots up a public place on American soil.

*   *   *   *   *

The Charlottesville, Virginia rampage by assorted white nationalist groups in August 2017 should have sounded loud the alarm bell that white nationalist and white supremacist groups have touched the delusional and loose wires in the heads of a more than a few impressionable, distraught, alienated, and unhinged, young white males. They have easy access to the big killer guns, and stocks of ammo, and bomb making parts. They are not routinely profiled by police. So, they can take pictures with guns, parade with guns publicly, and blast away at rifle ranges or at training sites. They have no fear of exposure or arrest.

The brutal reality, beyond the obvious issue of race and the political and religious typecasting of Muslims and Blacks, is there is simply no political incentive to call an Austin bomber a "domestic terrorist." This crashed hard against the official narrative that made-in-America terrorists and terrorism constitute minimal or no real threat to life and property here. This danger supposedly only comes from a foreign group, Muslim of course.

By any definition, Conditt was not just a domestic terrorist, but a racial terrorist. There is a bloody history that he was a part of. Scores of America first, neo-Nazis, and assorted overt racist groups have committed violence with impunity, and with a wink and nod from officials, judges, and police agencies on Blacks, Hispanics, and other outlier groups through much of American history. They, in effect, rewrote the definition of what terrorism is, and, isn't.

The resurgence of white nationalist groups and the hideous reports of their penetration into the armed forces and some police departments, has made it even harder to finger them as the same major threats to national security as is routinely true of Muslims from Syria, Iraq, Afghanistan, or Iran. Then when you had baby-faced school boys such as Conditt, and the litany of other white kid looking mass shooters and bombers, this made it impossible for the media and the public to rail against them as major threats to the nation's peace.

With their smiling, beatific faces, they simply look too much like the kid next door, the kid at a local school, or church, in white suburban communities. It would be too painful an exercise to turn the mirror inward and admit that that kid who many merely wrote off as an eccentric, a loner, or just a plain odd ball, could easily turn into a mass killer. Despite that grim reality the wall of denial that prevents an official admission that made-in-America terrorism can come with that smiling beatific, kid next door face, remains impregnable.

* * * * *

The Austin Bomber was the most dramatic and disturbing example of this failure to recognize that most domestic terror acts in America are committed by young whites. But there has been a steady parade of others that have been less dramatic, but deadly and that have also maimed and injured and traumatized communities. One of those, to illustrate, in which the two words "domestic" and "terrorist" were glaringly missing in the reams of news clips, press reports and news features was the case of the Colorado Springs Planned Parenthood Clinic killer, Robert Lewis Dear, in November 2015. His target, the clinic and his victims, were deliberately and calculatedly chosen. Then Attorney General Loretta Lynch promptly labeled the shooting a "crime against women receiving healthcare services at Planned Parenthood."

The shootings came against the backdrop of a months-long vicious, vile and relentless attack campaign vilifying Planned Parenthood by Republicans in efforts to gut, or outright eliminate, all funding for Planned Parenthood programs and services. The targets and the killings were, by any

definition, the lethal combination of politics and raw terrorism. Dear fit the classic profile, to a tee, of just who is likely
to commit a domestic terror act: namely a staunch gun advocate, politically disgruntled, white male.

Then President Obama, and then Democratic presidential contenders Hillary Clinton and Bernie Sanders, quickly
blasted the Colorado Springs mayhem. Yet, not one of the
GOP presidential contenders condemned the shootings, let
alone called the violence, domestic terrorism.

The issue of who gets called a domestic terrorist following a violent outburst exploded into national debate
following the massacre at the Charleston AME Church in
June 2015. Obama branded the massacre an act of terror.
Yet, nearly all major media outlets, and GOP leaders that
commented on it, and the FBI, absolutely refused to brand
the shooter, Dylann Roof, a terrorist or call his act an act of
domestic terrorism.

The refusal to call Roof or Dear, and others like them, a
"terrorist" is far from an arcane quibble over terms and defi-
nitions, or even over the race and gender of the shooters. It
strikes to the heart of how many Americans have been reflexively conditioned to see thuggery and terrorism. They see it
through the narrow, warped prism of who commits the acts,
rather than the horrific acts and their consequences.

Then FBI Director James B. Comey, for instance, was
blunt when pressed as to why he refused to brand Roof a terrorist: "Terrorism is an act done or threatened to in order to
try to influence a public body or the citizenry, so it's more of

a political act and then, again, based on what I know so far, I don't see it as a political act."

This begged the issue. In his so-called manifesto, Roof, by his own admission, made it clear that his target was Blacks and that he targeted them to sow fear and terror and start a racial conflagration.

Likewise, Dear made reference that he committed the terror act to stop the "killing of baby parts." This was very deliberate and pointed at specific groups that he saw as threats to the right-wing's stock definition of the American way. When you combine a hate-filled shooter's naming of groups, the easy access to guns and whatever demons are in his head, the horrid consequence is a terror act as sure as if he had mapped out a bomb attack on local Democratic Party headquarters.

The Justice Department did hint that it was exploring a domestic terrorism case against Roof. It subsequently did charge him with multiple federal hate crimes. He was convicted. Roof would also be prosecuted in state court. There was absolutely no guarantee, though, that state prosecutors would treat his act as anything other than a straight murder case. He subsequently pled guilty to nine counts of murder and was given a life sentence. Still, his alleged crime fit every definition of what a hate crime is in law and public policy as well as the classic definition of a terrorist act.

However, there's little doubt that if he had been Black and had shot up a Protestant church, he would have been branded a terrorist and the Justice Department would have been under relentless national pressure to bring terrorism charges against him. The act would have been a textbook legal fit of the FBI's definition of domestic terrorism which says it must be an act "dangerous to human life," that serves to "intimidate or coerce a civilian population."

Government agencies, much of the media and the broad segment of the public so far doggedly refuse to shed its ingrained mindset that terror acts can only be committed by a foreign group, almost always Muslim. This confuses, disarms and puts even more Americans in harm's way from the nation's real home-grown terrorists, who are likely to look, think, and act like Roof, Dear, and the Waco bikers.

CHAPTER 5

The Other Murders of Trayvon Martin and Michael Brown

In February 2012, 17-year-old Trayvon Martin was gunned down by the rogue, self-appointed vigilante George Zimmerman. The slaying of Martin and subsequent massive media attention to the slaying, and the trial and acquittal of Zimmerman was only part of the grim story. The other was what quickly happened the moment public attention began to focus on Martin. He was murdered again.

The second murder of Martin was the non-stop avalanche of veiled and not so veiled hints, innuendoes, digs, and crass, snide, accusing comments, remarks, slander and outright lies about his alleged bad background. Here were a few of the choice shots taken at Martin in the wake of the killing.

He had gold teeth. There were alleged Facebook defiant shots of him giving gang signs and flipping off. He was much bigger (and more menacing) than the stock angelic pictures of him. He had "non-violent behavioral issues in school." He was suspended for ten days, and his suspension may have been due to violence. He had tons of unexcused absences. He listened to rap and endlessly texted and talked on his cell phone.

Then the professional baiters and bashers took over. Fox Network's Gerald Rivera slurred that his Hoodie got him killed. TV and radio talker Glenn Beck branded him possibly a dangerous troublemaker. Just as predictably, then President Obama's sensitive and thoughtful statement of concern about Martin stirred a fresh round of Martin (and Obama) bashing up to and including GOP presidential contender Newt Gingrich. He accused the president of stirring up the racial pot by speaking out on the Martin murder.

The savage assault on Martin had two aims. One was to deconstruct him as supposedly not the innocent choir boy the press initially depicted him as. The even more devious and insidious aim was to exonerate Zimmerman for the murder. After all, if enough filth could be tossed at Martin to cast doubt and suspicion about his character and motives, then maybe Zimmerman had probable cause to kill.

The trashing of Martin as a closet thug was slanderous and silly stuff. The pantheon of stereotypes and negative typecasting it was anchored on was not. It was the shortest of short steps to think that if an innocent, in this instance, Martin, could be depicted as a caricature of the terrifying image that much of the public harbors about young Black males, then that image seemed real, even more terrifying, and the consequences were just as deadly.

*   *   *   *   *

Two and a half years year after the Martin killing, it happened again. This time the target was 18-year-old Michael Brown. Within hours after Brown was slain by Ferguson police officer, Darren Wilson, video footage was released from the convenience store that Brown had patronized in the moments before his confrontation with Wilson. That footage put Brown's life back in the public and media kill zone. It purported to show that he had committed a theft from the store in the moments before he was stopped by Wilson. This was more than enough to paint him as a thief, thug, and bad guy. The implication was that not only did Wilson have cause to confront Brown, but that the killing was justified.

The Brown slaying touched off weeks of unrest in Ferguson and other cities, a massive and prolonged federal probe, and a contentious, much watched and much debated, grand jury investigation that resulted in no charges being filed against Wilson. The slaying ignited a series of endless news reports, fierce debate and speculation, about just what kind of person Brown was. The release of the alleged incriminating video was just the start of the impugning of Brown. Police officials kicked into high gear with a loud, long, and vicious blame the victim campaign.

They held press conferences, and leaked documents. They orchestrated a well-oiled press campaign to depict

Brown as having gang ties, smoked dope, dealt dope, had an arrest record, was a school troublemaker, and engaged in every kind of deviant behavior, which included speculation that he was in the store to rob it. It was character assassination chock full of the stock racial stereotypes about young Black males. It firmly reinforced the public view that Brown was an outlaw who was up to no good when Wilson confronted him.

∗   ∗   ∗   ∗   ∗

The second slaying of Brown was the long delay in presenting evidence to the grand jury determining whether charges would be brought against Wilson. There was the careful tailoring and massaging by prosecutors of what the grand jury heard and saw about the circumstances of the killing. It reaffirmed the picture of Brown as a trouble-maker who posed a physical threat to Wilson and left the officer little choice but to kill in self-defense. This view was repeatedly buttressed by the evidence presented and the testimony of Wilson. There really was never much chance that a grand jury that was carefully led to believe the worst about Brown's actions would come to any other decision other than that Wilson acted properly and within the law.

St. Louis County Prosecutor Robert McCullough saw to that by using every legal maneuver under the sun to duck, dodge, and foot drag on convening a grand jury and charging it with determining whether Wilson should be indicted. Next, McCullough deliberately skewed, tainted, mangled, and even falsified, the evidence and testimony to hector the jurors into clearing Wilson. Then, when the inevitable happened, namely a non-indictment of Wilson, he grandstanded before the world to both slander Brown and pretend that his office would cooperate with the Justice Department in its probe. There was even a sickening footnote to this little charade. Wilson was paid a mini-ransom to go on national TV and play act that he, not Brown, was the poor victim of the whole sorry mess.

This didn't end the matter. The third slaying of Brown happened when the lead prosecutor piled on Brown by continuing to tar him as the aggressor and bad guy in the drama and defending Wilson's actions. Wilson was given free license to tell his side of the story in a highly-touted network TV interview.

This completed the enshrinement of Wilson as the true victim in the Brown saga and fully deserving of public sympathy and goodwill. This closed the door on the at best faint possibility that the Justice Department would file charges against Wilson. The case was officially closed when the Department brokered an agreement with Ferguson officials to revamp its police department's training and recruiting procedures. In March 2015, it made it official and announced that it would file charges against Wilson.

The decision not to indict Wilson ignited predictable anger, fury, more demonstrations, and a spasm of violence in Ferguson. This further reinforced the image of Brown, and those who supported him, as lawless and violent prone. At the same time, Brown became the symbol of the Black Lives

Matter movement and the impetus for a renewed movement against police violence against young Black males. This in turn cast Brown again as the poster figure in the acrimonious debate over police-black community conflict and further hardened the line between those who believe the police are under attack from the lawless and BLM protesters. This has had dire consequences.

A Stanford study released days before Brown's killing found that a significant number of whites and non-whites were even more willing to cheer tough sentencing, three strikes laws, and draconian drug busts, when they perceive that the majority of those busted and imprisoned are Black. In the months after the Brown slaying, the spiral of violence continued with the police slaying of Blacks in several cities, and the shocking murder of police officers in Dallas and Baton Rouge, Louisiana by Black shooters.

* * * * *

The murder of police officers by young Black males was no small point. Their tragic killings further reinforced the widespread public perception that police were under violent and serious attack from young Blacks. And they, not those Blacks who were the victims of police violence were the ones that should be lauded and deserved the sympathy and goodwill of the public. What was missed or deliberately ignored was that nearly every activist organization at the forefront of the protests over the killing of Brown, Eric Garner, Tamir Rice and Ezell Ford, as well as their family members, instantly condemned the killings of officers. Civil rights groups made it abundantly clear that anyone who tried to in any way intimate or justify the killings as some kind of retaliation or evening the score for the deaths of the Blacks killed was sick, a provocateur, and a vicious murderer.

Civil rights groups were emphatic that attacks on police officers are despicable and outrageous and reinforce the false and irresponsible notion that civil rights groups are anti-police. This outspoken condemnation of police officers slain was driven by both moral indignation and pragmatism. The great concern was that the killings could heighten tensions between police and Black communities, with even more deadly consequences for young Blacks. This is a potentially dangerous development, because an officer killing stirs anger, outrage, and fear among many police.

That could easily translate into more deadly encounters with officers driven by the fear that any and every young Black in any and every street or vehicle stop poses a danger to officers. This is when the stock racial stereotypes of young Blacks as violent threats could kick in and engender a potentially bad outcome.

Brown and Martin, were victims of police violence, as well as victims of the standard stereotypes of the dangerous Black male. They the price for that. The killing of police officers simply compounded the tragedy and erected fresh danger signs for both Blacks and the police.

CHAPTER 6

Turning Killers into All-Americans

The hideous slaying of second lieutenant Richard W. Collins III on the University of Maryland campus in May 2017, did more than evoke heartfelt grief and sorrow over the snuffing out of a young, hopeful, and high achieving young man's life. It also again cast the ugly glare on the gaping double standard in how Black lives matter versus those of white lives. Let's go through the agonizing, but by now all too familiar, checklist of things that were terribly wrong with how his death was treated.

First, there was the alleged assailant, Sean Urbanski, a young white man. The tributes to Collins had barely poured out at Bowie State University, where he was days from graduating, when Urbanski's attorney not only pled innocence for his client, but implored the court to release him on own recognizance, provide alcohol and drug testing counseling, and monitor him during his release by GPS. The request was denied. But it might not have been since judges in other controversial cases where young white males have been accused of crimes from rape to murder have been given bail, and the most lenient of supervision requirements pending their trial.

This is exactly what happened to 18-year-old white teen, Cameron Terrell, from an affluent family who was charged with murder for the gang-related killing of a 21-year-old man in October 2017 in Los Angeles. Terrell got bail and was spotted with his parents later at a Dodgers baseball game. Terrell's bail release despite a capital charge got only cursory attention in the press. His case was no aberration. A study by MassINC, an independent Boston think tank, in 2015, looked at pretrial detention in 10 Massachusetts counties. It found that whites were four times more likely to be granted bail than Black and Hispanic defendants.

Prosecutors quickly denounced the study as not taking into account mitigating factors, the most important being the severity of the crime. However, even agreeing that Black and Hispanic defendants committed more serious crimes than whites, the gaping disparity was still far to great to simply air brush this away as a case of there being more serious mitigating circumstances that kept Blacks arrested locked up before trial while whites walked. This was especially true since no proof was presented to show that white offenders were committing crimes that were any less serious than those committed by Blacks

* * * * *

Then there were the charges against Urbanski. He was charged with first degree murder. So far so good. However, the irrefutable fact was that Collins was African-American, and Urbanski is white. He had a documented connection with an Alt Reich- Nation Facebook group, and there was absolutely no evidence of any provocation on the part of Collins to precipitate the murder. His tie to an Alt-Reich group was sloughed off as just a light hearted, silly, fun and games, attempt by some college guys to draw attention to the group. The founder of the group was given tons of ink to make the case that spewing racism and white nationalism was the furthest thing from the minds of those associated with the group, and presumably that included Urbanski,

Then there is Urbanski. He was immediately depicted by friends and associates as a quiet, assuming, even good-natured fellow, who couldn't hurt a fly. All expressed shock and surprise that this seemingly good natured, all-American, clean cut good guy could commit such a dastardly crime.

This again fit the standard pattern whether it's a single act of violence, or mass terror act. When the perpetrator is white the hunt is immediately on to "explain" him and his actions. This in effect humanizes him, almost his act too, and invariably engenders at best, an attempt to understand his motives, and at its grotesque worst, warped sympathy, even compassion for him. An especially macabre example of that was the avalanche of letters, well-wish cards, and even money that poured into the Boward County jail for Nicholas Cruz.

Now Cruz was sitting in a jail cell after being charged with the murder of 17 persons at Marjory Stoneman Douglas High School in February 2018 and faced the death penalty. The throng cheered him on as if he was part rock star, and part All-American boy, not a monster killer. This didn't surprise. He got the same hearts and flowers description in the flood of news clips, press reports and news features as other young white males who maim and murder. He was "troubled," "a loner," 'hostile," and "no clue he was dangerous." His defense attorneys piled on to this litany of descriptive cop-outs by calling him "brain damaged," "emotionally traumatized," and the topper, "a broken child (He's 19, that's hardly a child). Then Trump jumped in with the by now stock characterizations reserved for white mass killers, as "mentally disturbed," "bad and erratic behavior," and with what's hardly the revelation of the ages, "a big problem." As always, the two words that were glaringly and embarrassingly missing in labeling Cruz, were "domestic' and "terrorist."

✶ ✶ ✶ ✶ ✶

The routine characterization of Cruz or an Urbanski as "troubled" and "disturbed" was not a small point. The image massage of men such as them is almost tantamount to likening them to a bunch of harmless, fun loving, thrill-seeking college students. This almost takes off the table the charge that Urbanski murdered Collins out of racial malice. In other words, that the murder was a hate crime and he should be charged under state or federal law as a hate crime perpetrator.

The Prince George's County Attorney expressed doubt and hesitancy about the motive. For months the Justice Department was stone silent on whether it would consider a separate hate crime prosecution of Urbanski. Later it did slap a hate crime charge on him. But this was the rare exception in cases such as this. The argument was always why bring a hate crime charge in these cases, even if there is a racial intent? The assailant is already being charged with and will be tried on a first-degree murder count.

This badly skirted the question. A hate crime enhancement in racial assaults and murders is on the books as a deterrent and punishment to racially motivated assaults and murder. The failure to bring hate crimes charges sends the dangerous message that hate crimes, especially hate murders, will not be punished as racially driven hate crimes, but won't even be called that even when there is compelling evidence they are. And the incidences of hate crimes have shown no sign of diminishing. Year in and year out, the FBI's annual reports on hate crime violence in America report thousands of them. There are probably thousands more that aren't reported. African-Americans are still the prime target of hate crime attacks. A murder charge and a conviction in racially motivated hate attacks and murders alone is hardly a disincentive stern to curb hate crimes.

There is also evidence that white nationalist, white supremacist groups and the social media ravings of kooky unhinged hate mongers hold a perverse fascination for many white students on college campuses. Since Trump's election in November 2016, a CBS report found nearly 150 incidences of racist posters and fliers on college campuses in nearly three dozen states.

However, even before Trump's election ushered in a new era of hate, intolerance, and bigotry, hardly a week went by without a report somewhere of hanging nooses, white hoods, racist graffiti, racial slurs and taunts aimed at minority students. The colleges that have been called on the carpet for the racist acts read like a who's who of American higher education. Clemson University, Auburn, Lehigh, Tarleton State, Texas A&M, University of Texas, Austin, University of Connecticut, Johns Hopkins, Whitman College, the University of Oklahoma, U.C.L.A., U.C. San Diego, and the University of Maryland, to name only a very handful. The Harvard University Voices of Diversity project found campuses rife with subtle and not-so-subtle "microaggressions" against minority and women students.

The final insults in the Collins slaying case was that he, and it, quickly disappeared from the headlines. That there was an initial hesitation, doubt, and apparent reluctance of officials to call racial hate, racial hate even when it's murder, and the victim is Black told much about the ambivalence and deep reluctance on the part of prosecutors to call racially motivated murder, just that. And when the perpetrator is a young white male, a major effort is made to understand him. Unfortunately, that same public grasp for understanding is rarely there when the perpetrator is are young black men such as Richard Collins III.

CHAPTER 7

The School-to-Prison Pipeline

In 1999, the U.S. Department of Education found that Black students were getting the boot from schools far faster and in much bigger numbers than white students. While Blacks made up then less than 20 percent of the nation's public school students, they comprised nearly one out of three students kicked out of the schools. Things were so bad then that the NAACP held public hearings nationally on the racial disparities in school discipline. The hearings were timely and needed. However, they didn't change anything.

Nearly two decades later, a Department of Education survey on racial disparities in public education found that Black students were still getting the boot from schools faster than any other group, and that included Black females, who were disproportionately suspended and expelled more than white females from schools. There were two new wrinkles this time. The Department found that the students were getting suspended in astoundingly disproportionate numbers even before they ever set foot in a regular school classroom. According to figures, nearly 50 percent of preschoolers who received more than one suspension were Black. This was double that of white students, though Blacks made up less than 20 percent of public school preschoolers.

If that wasn't bad enough even putting a Black child in a charter school and even with a disability, was no safe haven. The Center for Civil Rights Remedies in a 2016 study found that Black disabled students at these schools were twice as likely to be suspended or expelled as white disabled students.

No matter what age they were suspended or expelled, the students were far more likely to wind up in police stations and courtrooms after removal. This cast an even harsher glare on the stiff punishment school officials routinely dished out to Black students who allegedly misbehave. It was no overreach or apology for misconduct to say "allegedly" about the reasons for their suspensions, expulsions and often arrest. Teams of academics closely examined the notion that Black students were more violent, disruptive or menacing than white students. They found that the disparities in suspensions didn't result from Blacks "acting out" in the classroom more than whites. The heavy-handed ouster of Black students from schools was also a major factor in the grossly high dropout rate of Black students from many inner-city schools.

Many teachers and administrators expel and suspend

more Black students than white students, and school officials and district attorneys prosecute them in greater numbers, because of racial fear, ignorance and the ease in getting convictions of, and plea bargains from them. When some young Blacks turned to gangs, guns, and drugs and terrorized their communities, much of the press titillated the public with endless features on the crime-prone, crack-plagued, blood-stained streets of the ghetto. TV action news crews turned into a major growth industry, stalking Black neighborhoods, filming busts for the nightly news. The explosion of gangster rap and the spate of Hollywood ghetto films convinced many Americans that the thug lifestyle was the Black lifestyle. They had ghastly visions of young Blacks menacing their neighborhoods.

In addition, school principals have near dictatorial power. They set the standards of what is acceptable behavior or not, and once that's done and a student is deemed a discipline problem, there isn't much parents can do to reverse a decision to suspend or expel. In fact, studies have found that poor and minority parents are less likely than white, middle-class parents to challenge school officials decisions to suspend or expel their children.

* * * * *

There are two other reasons that school officials grossly overreact to the real or perceived bad behavior of some Black students. The federal Gun-Free Schools Act, passed in 1994, requires that states order their schools to kick students out for weapons possession in order to qualify for federal funds. (School officials later expanded the list of violations for student expulsion to include fighting and other violent acts.) California's zero-tolerance school laws, for instance, mandate that a student be expelled for one year for infractions that include drug sales, robbery, assault, weapons possession and fights that cause serious physical injury. The only exception is if the student that caused the injury acted in self-defense.

The horrific stories of students wielding guns and knives on campuses and assaulting and terrorizing other students have deepened public panic that murderous youths are running amok at schools. School officials zealously enforce get-tough policies to prove that they will do whatever it takes to get rid of disruptive students. The danger is that school officials that reflexively view young Blacks as violence-prone, menace-to-society thugs have turned zero-tolerance into a repressive tool that victimizes black students.

As the survey showed, the quick-trigger suspension and expulsion of Black students from schools at the drop of a dime has reached down into preschools and preconditioned far too many teachers and principals to regard Black children who are barely removed from the crib as classroom dangers. The end result was that the school-to-prison pipeline became even more unyielding and socially damaging because it starts at an even earlier age. This would end only when school officials stop the racial profiling of Black students, and that first and foremost now included Black children.

The focus has been intense on the wildly disproportionate

number of Black students who are suspended or expelled from America's public schools. But what has flown quietly under the radar is the even more wildly disproportionate number of Black students who are arrested on high school and even elementary school campuses for alleged behavior that in decades past was handled in the principal's office and with a call home to parents. That's still the way school infractions are handled with most white students and in most suburban public schools.

If the student is Black, a cross word between students, a glare at the teacher, or a scuffle is likely to bring the police. The hard numbers tell the brutal tale of the iron fist treatment of Blacks by school administrators. The U.S. Department of Education's Office of Civil Rights in separate reports in 2012 and 2014 found that more than 70 percent of Black and Hispanic students were involved in school related arrests or simply turned over to local police and the courts. The report found that the actual arrest rate for Black students was one-third higher than for white students.

In the Chicago public schools in 2011 the number of black students arrested even topped the national average. Nearly three-quarters of all arrests were of African-American students though they comprised less than half of the Chicago public school students. They were arrested at a rate nearly four times higher than even that of Latinos. Chicago is no exception. The racially disproportionate number of arrests for Black and white students could be found in other big city school districts with a sizeable Black student population. The disproportionate arrest figure for Black students in Chicago in 2011 has held fairly steady every year since.

School officials defend their quick resort to call in the school or city police with the claim that Black students do commit more serious offenses than other students. There is nothing to support this. The overwhelming majority of the arrests are not for serious offenses such as robbery, assault, or gang violence, but for offenses such as disrespect, excessive noise, threatening behavior and loitering. White students by contrast were punished for infractions that could be clearly documented such as smoking, vandalism and using obscene language. The other behavior was strictly a subjective call by the teacher or school administrator.

In January 2013, then Attorney General Eric Holder alarmed at the trend toward lock em' up first for any and all infractions by Black students urged school districts to rethink their zero-tolerance discipline policies and the detrimental effect it was having on the education of far too many students. Some school districts tried to ease back the throttle on the rushing in the police for any and every infraction in the classroom or on school grounds. They reverted to treating minor discipline problems as problems to be handled at the school administrative level. This was welcome. Yet, there were far too many school officials who zealously enforced get-tough policies to prove that they would do whatever it takes to get rid of disruptive students.

The problem with that is that those students are and remain mostly Black. Trump's grab of the White House in

2016, promised that things would get worse. His Education Secretary, Betsy DeVos made clear that she didn't believe a word of the reports that Black students were profiled in public schools, and that they were ousted for anything other than bad behavior that merited their ouster.

She wasted no time once in office in trying to scrap the Obama administration issued guidance in 2014 that urged schools to examine the disproportionate rates at which Black students were being punished. DeVos barged ahead with her effort to dump the guidance protocol even after a report from the Government Accountability Office in April 2018 that again found that Black students were given the boot from schools and arrested far faster and more often than white students. The irony is that the Obama guidance to school districts on taking measures to reduce the racial disparities in school discipline was just that a guidance, meaning that it was left up to the school districts to take action, or not. To DeVos even a tepid measure such as that was too much to stomach.

*   *   *   *   *

There was yet one more blowback from the heavy-handed near criminalization of Black school kids. That was the strong push to turn schools into armed camps. The ridiculous and terrifying sight of dozens of police dressed and packing assault-style weapons as if they had just stepped out of a combat zone in Iraq or Afghanistan in Ferguson, Missouri following the mass protests over the police slaying of Michael

Brown was horrifying enough. Now an increasing number of America's school police were packing the same semiautomatic weapons.

School districts in dozens of cities approved the use of these types of weapons for campus police. One district, the almost exclusively Black and Hispanic Compton, California school district drew headline news in 2015 when it joined the parade of school districts that authorized its police to pack these high caliber battlefield-style killing weapons. The danger and absurdity of school officials' rush to arm their school police to the teeth is that there was absolutely no need for these weapons.

The Bureau of Justice Statistics did a 10-year study, from 2002 to 2011, of mass shootings in America. It found that less than one-fifth of one percent of all shootings in the country involved four or more victims. Let's fine tune this more. Noted criminologist James Alan Fox examined the numbers on shootings on all school campuses in the nation and found that less than one percent of all shootings involved multiple victims. Let's fine tune the numbers even more: the Centers for Disease Control, in two separate reports on K-12 school shootings, found that the chance of a child dying in school in any given year from a homicide or suicide was less than one in one million in the early 1990s and one in two million in the later 1990s. This probability has remained unchanged in the decade since. The numbers and percentages tell one glaring fact. Despite the horror, hysteria, and media sensationalism over the Newtown and Columbine massacres in 2012 and

1999, mass shootings in America's schools are not just rare, but rarer than ever.

There has been no reported mass shooting at any school in any predominantly Black or Hispanic neighborhood in the country ever. Yet, despite the overwhelming evidence that an AR-15 poses a grave threat to all who handle or come within its striking range, more than a few school boards have still barged ahead to allow its school police to arm themselves with these weapons of mass killings. They tore a page straight out of the playbook the NRA has used to beat back any congressional effort to ban assault weapons and claimed that they give cops a weapon to take out the bad guy presumably faster and more permanent in a shoot-out on a school campus.

The heavy-handed overkill by the poorly trained, battlefield armed police in Ferguson, Missouri prompted then President Obama and even the Pentagon to promise to review the military's wholesale giveaway of a dizzying array of tanks, body armor, and assault-style weapons to big and small city police department. Obama was rightly aghast that the gobbling up by police departments of weapons of mass destruction had gotten way out of hand and the nation had taken a dangerous step toward the establishment of a full blown national security state that posed a mortal threat to the lives and constitutional rights of Americans.

In ordering his review of the military weapons programs, Obama said "there is a big difference between our military and our local law enforcement and we don't want to blur those lines." School officials that have armed their police with assault-style weapons have done more than blur that line. They have sent the horrific message that weapons of mass destruction have a place at their schools. That message was eagerly embraced by Trump. He grossly over-reacted to the horror and the mania following the massacre at a Parkland, Florida High School in February 2018 by demanding that teachers be allowed to pack guns on K-12 campuses. This silly, preposterous call, was fraught with peril for students and teachers. Even more ominously, many of those schools were in the poorest of poor, Black communities. And the students at those schools would be watched just as intently and warily as if they were battlefield enemies.

CHAPTER 8

Why Cops Who Kill Walk Free

Samuel DuBose, Sylville Smith, Philando Castile, and Terence Crutcher. These were four Black men who were slain by police in three cities at four different times between 2015 and 2017. The circumstances in all four cases, though, were, eerily the same. The killings came after stops by the officers. The men apparently posed no physical threat to the officers. Two were shot while running away. The other two were shot in their cars. There was chilling video footage of the killings. The only twist in the shootings was that two of the officers who were not convicted, one was a mistrial, were not white cops. One was Black, the other Hispanic. All four were either acquitted or there was a mistrial.

The non-convictions of the cops brought the scorecard on police shootings of those Black men, to 0 out of 4. That was just the latest in the grim count of unsuccessful prosecutions in dubious police shootings of Blacks in the rare times that cops were hauled into a criminal courtroom. Rare, because there are about 1000 police shootings in the U.S. each year, with Blacks three times more likely to die from use of force by officers than whites.

The police killings of Black men, who in most of the cases were unarmed, and the non-convictions of the cops who kill them has become not only a common-place, but expected. It makes no difference whether there's a video that shows beyond any question that the victims posed no threat to the officers, had no weapon, or were shot from a distance, often in the back. The universal shout is that the killings and the acquittals of the police who kill them are simply more proof that the system is violent, racist, and hateful of Black men whose lives have no value. That is certainly true when the deadly mix of fear, stereotypes, high crime, and poor training, clash when many officers encounter a young Black male in a poor inner-city neighborhood.

The propensity of many police officers to shoot first and ask questions later (if at all) was borne out even before they were faced with a real-life target in a Black neighborhood. *The Journal of Experimental Social Psychology* published a study by researchers from the University of Illinois at Urbana-Champaign in 2015 that found that people were much more likely to shoot at a Black target than at a white target

The study concluded, "Because these associations reside outside of conscious awareness and control, even well-meaning, consciously egalitarian officers are vulnerable to use more force on minority civilians, "Police officers are only human, and in use-of-force situations they experience the kinds of normal emotions—fear, anger, anxiety—that set the stage for more spontaneous mental processes to be influential."

* * * * *

However, that didn't tell why cops have virtually a guaranteed walk free pass from judges, juries, and prosecutors the rare times that they do wind up in a court docket in the killing of a young Black. The reason for that tells much about the way the over use of deadly force by officers is treated within the criminal justice system. The starting point is the decision to prosecute the officer. There are two absolute indispensable elements for that to happen. One, the video footage of the killing that appears to show beyond any doubt that the officer wantonly killed the suspect. The other is that there is mass public outrage, protests, or even the threat of violent disruptions, if there isn't a prosecution. Even then, prosecutors tread very deliberately and warily, knowing that getting a conviction is a fierce uphill slog. The defense attorneys for the accused cops make that a certainty.

They are among the best in the defense trial business with lots of experience defending police officers accused of misconduct. Police unions bankroll their defense and spare no expense. The officers are immediately bailed out and they will serve no actual pre-trial jail time.

Their defense attorneys have three time tested legal ploys. One is they play for time. They know that memories dim and passions cool, and the cases quickly drop from public and media focus. They file countless motions demanding the charges be dropped or reduced. They'll occasionally demand a change of venue. In each case, the time clock is running in the case.

They often seek a bench trial, but when that is denied, no matter, the clock is still running pending a decision. If the case goes to jury, defense attorneys seek to get as many middle-class people, whites and even Blacks and Latinos, on the jury as possible. The presumption is that they are much more likely to believe the testimony of police and police defense witnesses than Black witnesses, defendants, or even the victims. Another hurdle are judges, or rather the often subtle, and implicit, racial bias of many judges. The power of a judge to show mercy or throw the book at a defendant is well-documented. However, far murkier and ambiguous is just how much the racial attitudes and views of judges color their sentencing decisions.

Two university researchers in 2012 tested just how racial bias determines whether a judge will slap a long prison stretch on a defendant or give a defendant the kid glove treatment. The researchers were careful to control for similarities of the crimes, and backgrounds of the defendants, the quality of their attorneys, the attitudes of the defendants, and most importantly the prior criminal history of the defendants. This is crucial because one of the counter arguments to the charge of the racial double standard in sentencing is that Blacks are more likely to have a longer rap sheet than whites, and judges must take that into consideration.

They examined cases based on the randomness in which judges are assigned cases to assure that there was a large enough sample of cases. This meant that on average that judges would get the same types of cases with the same mix of defendants and crimes. The study found that judges in most cases were far more likely to give a Black defendant a harsher sentence than a white defendant. This markedly increased both the incarceration rate for Blacks and the length of their sentence.

* * * * *

There's yet another reason why judges are more prone to give hand slap sentences to a police officer convicted in an overuse of deadly force case while throwing the book at a Black defendant. It comes down to how a judge sees a defendant even before he or she becomes a defendant. Judges are human and susceptible to the same biases, prejudices, and swallowing of stereotypes as anyone else. Countless tests of implicit racial bias have shown that many whites view Blacks as more threatening, menacing, and crime prone than whites. The implicit bias is there even when judges to all appearances make every effort to appear fair and unbiased toward a defendant.

Yet there are many points during the process that it can come in. Judges make decisions on bail, pretrial motions, evidentiary issues, witness credibility, jury selection, and instructions to the jury. Judges also can and do weigh the status of the defendant in the community, and the support that he or she gets from outsiders. When fellow police officers show up in court to support an officer on trial in a misconduct case, this has got to have an affect on judges as well as jurors.

*   *   *   *   *

A judge's willingness to bend over backwards toward a defendant or to be tough is deeply influenced by prosecutors. Studies have found that they are more likely to charge Blacks with crimes that carry minimum sentences and give the judge little or no room to exercise their discretion in sentencing. This almost never happens with a cop who has been convicted in a use of force case.

The negative perceptions of Blacks, especially Black males, by much of the public is a major problem. Yet, almost as daunting is that there is no ironclad standard of what is or isn't an acceptable use of force in police killings. It comes down to a judgment call by the officer. The time-tested standard that is virtually encoded in law is that "I feared for my life." This will be stated, massaged, and repeated in every conceivable way by defense attorneys during their presentation. They'll bolster that by painting a vivid and fearful picture of the defendant as violent and aggressive. The message being that the use of deadly force was both necessary and justified.

The cases often hinge heavily on the video footage that will prove beyond a shadow of a doubt that the officer overused deadly force. It does no such thing. Defense attorneys twist, turn, dissect, re-dissect, analyze and reanalyze the footage from every earthly angle. They claim that it really doesn't show what led up to the slaying, doesn't fully show the danger to the officer, doesn't show the officers giving instructions to him to comply, and is too limited in the angle that it was shot. They will have a use of force and a technical expert testify to the validity of that claim. It's still a matter of what you see is not what you see in these cases.

Following the slaying of Stephon Clark, and unarmed young Black man, by Sacramento police in March 2018, a group of California state legislators were so incensed that they proposed bills that mandated that officers could only use deadly force when absolutely necessary. Specifically, that meant only to prevent imminent and serious bodily injury or death, and only after all non-lethal de-escalation tactics were used to subdue a suspect. Police unions immediately attacked the bills or suggested major revisions.

So, that tossed the ball again back to prosecutors. They know the odds are stacked against them in convicting cops who kill because of those odds. The shut out in convicting the cops who killed Smith, Dubose, Castile and Crutcher did nothing to change those odds. This doesn't mean, though, that prosecutors shouldn't try. A prosecution, even a failed prosecution, would still send the strong signal that the wanton killing of unarmed Blacks will not be ignored both in law and public policy.

CHAPTER 9

Poor Black Women = Cheap Black Lives

In March 2017, the Congressional Black Caucus a letter to Attorney General Jeff Sessions and then FBI Director James Comey, asking that they "devote the resources necessary to determine whether these developments are an anomaly, or whether they are indicative of an underlying trend that must be addressed. (W)hen children of color go missing, authorities often assume they are runaways rather than victims of abduction." The CBC was being polite and diplomatic in the calling the alarm among Black D.C. residents over the rising number of missing Black girls in D.C. which by the time the CBC wrote the letter had jumped to more than a dozen. Their cases had garnered little national media and public attention.

Because of that the media and Washington D.C. police

and city officials were hammered for allegedly ignoring the plight of the missing Black and Latina girls in Washington D.C. Community activists chalked the seeming indifference up to racism. The outcry triggered a spate of news stories on the missing girls, angry denials from the police that they were asleep on the job in trying to find the girls, and lots of stats that purported to show that there's been no major uptick in the number of missing persons in the District, and certainly nothing that points to any conspiracy to nab, traffic in, or murder young Black females.

The push back against the charges of murder and conspiracy was almost certainly right. However, it didn't answer the perennial question about how Black female lives versus the lives of white females in distress are viewed and treated. The CBC gingerly hinted at one aspect of that difference when it said that authorities downplay missing Black girls while regarding white girls who turn up missing as victims of a heinous crime complete with non-stop headlines and coverage.

The gaping disparity in the number of Black kids missing, and how their disappearance is treated, is certainly glaring. According to FBI figures in 2016, African-American children made up 42 percent of non-family abductions. Yet, one would be hard pressed to find amber alert tweets and their pictures plastered on freeway alert signs. The media was no better. A 2010 Pace University study compared reporting by race and gender on several major news stations between 2005 and 2007. Predictably, it found that Black kids were almost invisible in news coverage.

The issue of which victims get covered and ignored exploded as a major racial crisis issue when several cities were hit with a wave of serial murders of Black women during the 1980s. The shout was that the murders went on with no public warning, media coverage, and seemingly scant police action for years. Police and prosecutors each time bristled at the charge that they were less diligent when it came to nailing serial killers who kill Blacks than whites.

In Los Angeles which had a serial killer roaming on the loose in the 1980s killing scores of mostly poor Black women, officials pleaded that they were under staffed, lacked the resources, and technology to make a swift arrest when the killings began. There was some truth to that then. But since then there's been a tremendous advance in the use of computer matches, and forensic and DNA testing. This helped police quickly zero in on likely suspects. In Los Angeles, police officials went further and set-up special task forces to track down the killer.

* * * * *

That still begged the question that lurked underneath the case of D.C.'s missing girls. That is that far too often police and city officials do not see victims in inner city neighborhoods as the type of women who reflexively ignite police and public outrage. There are reasons, troubling reasons, for this.

Poor black women have from time immemorial been hammered by racial and gender stereotypes, criminal violence, and toss-away-the-key punitive laws.

Their grotesque treatment has had horrific consequences.

• *Cheap life:* East St. Louis, Illinois for instance, in 2000, made news when FBI agents implored police officials in the city to allow their serial killer unit help hunt down the suspected serial killer of five women in the city. Police officials flatly turned them down. It was not the first time the FBI offered to help them catch the murderer, and each time they said no. They gave no public explanation why they refused FBI help. 1½ years later, with the grisly body count climbing to 13 murders the city finally relented and the FBI joined in the hunt for the killer. The initial refusal of city officials to get the FBI involved underscored the colossal risk of murder and criminal violence more Black women faced. Homicide ranked as a major cause of death for young Black females. A Black woman is ten times likelier to be raped and assaulted than a white woman. The media often magnifies and sensationalizes crimes by Black men against white women and ignores or downplays crimes against black women.

• *Drug menace:* In 1999, a handful of Black U.S. Customs Service agents blew the whistle on the abusive treatment of Black women air travelers. They revealed that thousands of Black women travelers were subject to illegal strip searches, x-ray examinations, monitored bowel movements, unlawful detentions, and targeted monitoring by drug sniffing dogs in their search for drug traffickers.

This stirred a national furor and tossed the odious light on the mounting numbers of women, especially Black women, arrested for illegal drug use.

- **Dangerous women:** The police slayings of Black women in Los Angeles, Riverside, California, and Chicago, D.C. and other cities over the years, and a sharp upswing in violent crimes by women, and Hollywood films that show Black women as swaggering, trash talking, gun-toting, vengeful Thelma and Louise types, have escalated public fears that Black women are menaces to society. The result: One in four women are now imprisoned for violent crimes, and half of them are Black. Also, in some surveys, many Black women have complained that they, as many Black men, are racially profiled.

- **Skyrocketing imprisonment:** Black women are eight times likelier to be jailed than white women. Black women in some states are imprisoned at nearly the same rate as white men. And they are being jailed at even younger ages than ever. An American Bar Association in 2017 found that teen girls account for more than one-quarter of the juvenile arrests, are committing more violent crimes, and are slapped back into detention centers after release faster than boys. Black girls were arrested and jailed in far greater numbers than white girls. Almost certainly many of these delinquent teen girls will jam America's prisons as women.

* * * * *

The long running serial killing saga of Black women as typified by the East St. Louis murders underscored the great threat of murder and criminal violence to many Black women. That's only one menace. Nearly half of the women behind bars in America are there for drug-related offenses, the majority are Black. Some of the suspected serial murder victims, and in some instances in the case of D.C.s missing girls, had a rap sheet for drug use, trafficking, or simply hailed from troubled homes. This was repeatedly mentioned in press accounts of the victims. They easily fit the popular public and media profile of the drugged-out, derelict Black woman.

The American Bar Association conducted studies that found that teen girls account for more than one-quarter of the juvenile arrests, are committing more violent crimes, and are slapped back into detention centers after release faster than boys. Black girls were arrested and jailed in far greater numbers than white girls.

The proactive steps taken by D.C. police, city officials, and the Congressional Black Caucus which called for federal intervention in the hunt for the missing girls were welcome and much needed. It certainly made the public much more aware of the peril that many Black girls and women face on the streets; and part of that peril is the possibility of being the victim of violence.

The big danger remained, though, that official casualness toward the murders could translate into more bodies. This would again confirm the suspicion that when the victims are poor, Black and female, their lives are cheap, and expendable.

* * * * *

By far the greatest hazard to Black women is imprisonment. Some years ago I briefly worked as a social worker.

Occasionally I would visit clients in jail to determine their eligibility for continued benefits. They were all men—with one exception. She was a young Black woman serving time for theft. She had two small children.

She entered the visiting room handcuffed to another woman and dressed in drab prison garb. We talked through a reinforced glass window. The guards stared hard and barked out gruff commands to the women. This was in the 1980s. The idea of a woman in prison then was a novelty. By 2018, it wasn't. According to Justice Department reports on America's jail population, women make up about 10 percent of the America's inmates. There are now more women than ever serving time, and Black women make up a disproportionate number of those women. They are twice more likely than Hispanic, and over three times more likely than white women, to be jailed.

In fact, Black women have almost single-handedly expanded the women's prison-industrial complex. From 1930 to 1950 five women's prisons were built nationally. During the 1980s and 1990s dozens more prisons were built, and a growing number of them were maximum-security women's prisons. The prison-building splurge didn't keep pace with the swelling number of women prisoners. Women's prisons are understaffed, overcrowded, lack recreation facilities, serve poor quality food, suffer chronic shortages of family planning counselors and services, and gynecological specialists, drug treatment and child care facilities, and transportation funds for family visits.

Female prisoners face the added peril of rape, and

insensitive treatment during pregnancy. Reports have found that more than two dozen states in 2018 permitted pregnant women to be shackled while being transported to hospitals for treatment. A report by the National Corrections Information Center revealed that the U.S. is one of only a handful of countries that allow men to guard women, often unsupervised. Author Donna Ann-Smith Marshall, who served several years at Central California Women's Facility, California's top maximum security prison, in her book, *Time on the Inside: Behind the Walls in a Maximum Security Women's Prison, from an Insider's View,* told in shocking and graphic detail the callous, often brutal treatment many women are subjected to in women's maximum security jails.

More Black women are behind bars as much because of hard punishment than their actual crimes. One out of three crimes committed by women are drug related. Many state and federal sentencing laws mandate minimum sentences for all drug offenders. This virtually eliminates the option of referring non-violent first-time offenders to increasingly scarce, financially strapped drug treatment, counseling and education programs. Stiffer punishment for crack cocaine use also has landed more Black women in prison, and for longer sentences than white women (and men).

Then there's the feminization of poverty and racial stereotyping. More than one out of three Black women jailed did not complete high school, were unemployed, or had incomes below the poverty level at the time of their arrest. More than half of them were single parents.

While black men are typed as violent, drug dealing gangsters, Black women are typed as sexually loose, conniving, untrustworthy, or welfare queens. Many of the mostly middle-class judges and jurors believe that Black women offenders are menaces to society too.

* * * * *

The quantum leap in the number of Black women behind bars has had devastating impact on families and the quality of life in many poor Black communities. Thousands of children of incarcerated women are raised by grandparents or warehoused in foster homes and institutions. The children are frequently denied visits because the mothers are deemed unfit. This prevents mothers from developing parenting and nurturing skills and deeply disrupts the parent-child bond. Many children of imprisoned women drift into delinquency, gangs, and drug use. This perpetuates the vicious cycle of poverty, crime, and violence. There are many cases where parents and even grandparents are jailed.

For a Black woman that has served her time and been released, the roadblocks toward getting back on her feet again are still massive. The most grueling is finding a job. The myth that Black women who have been jailed have a decided advantage over Black men when it comes to finding a job is just that a myth. The instant an employer finds that a woman has a criminal or arrest record the door for employment frequently slams shut on her. Without a job, and the slender prospects of getting one, this is a virtual pipeline back to the streets and the heightened risk again of incarceration. The cycle of arrest, jail, and release, and re-imprisonment just keeps repeating itself for many Black women.

There is little sign that this will change. The public and policy makers are deeply trapped in the damaging cycle of myths, misconceptions, and crime fear hysteria about crime-on-the-loose women, especially Black women. They are loath to ramp up funds and programs for job and skills training, drug treatment, education, childcare and health, and parenting skills. This is still the best way to keep more Black women from winding up behind bars. It's those same negative myths and stereotypes about Black women and crime that present a formidable barrier to implementing those much-needed policy changes.

CHAPTER 10

Even Money Can't Buy a Racial Pass

In his 2006 book, *The Audacity of Hope*, former President Obama ticked off the standard checklist of slights and abuses that he had routinely faced over the years: security guards tailing him as he shopped in department stores, white couples who tossed him their car keys as he stood outside a restaurant waiting for the valet, police cars pulling him over for no apparent reason. Obama noted that he was subjected to these slights and insults during his college days and even after he launched his professional career.

A year after Obama's election in 2008, New York Congressman Charles Rangel cracked that if Obama strolled through East Harlem at nightfall sans suit, presidential entourage and limo, he could be shaken down, spread-eagled, and cuffed. Rangel took much heat for a seemingly impertinent and ridiculous quip and walked it back—but as Obama strongly hinted in his book, and his very empathetic remarks on the slaying of Trayvon Martin in 2012 about the plight of young Black males, Rangel wasn't too far off the mark in zeroing in on the endemic problem of racial profiling.

Former US Attorney General Eric Holder also later told his tale of being pulled over twice as a college student driving on the New Jersey Turnpike and again as a federal prosecutor in Washington D.C. Their point was clear. Obama, the college student and professional, and Holder, the federal prosecutor, were not immune from the harassment, targeting, possible arrest, and even in some cases, violence while walking or driving while Black. Obama and Holder happened to be the most glaring, and to some, surprising examples of a Black professional or academic subject to police abuse. Legions of prominent blacks have had the same or worse experiences.

There are no figures or studies made on just how many prominent African-Americans have been subject to abuse in public places by police when there was absolutely no evidence that a crime had been committed. Yet, in the aftermath of the slaying of Martin, many prominent Blacks bared their chest publicly about being embarrassed, harassed, and assailed by police, private security guards, storeowners, and clerks. Their names read like a who's who of the wealthiest and biggest names among Blacks.

The susceptibility of even celebrated Black men to be hauled off when there's even the slightest suspicion, mistaken or otherwise, of criminal wrongdoing has left many police officials red-faced with embarrassment when they realized their goof. This was the case with celebrated tennis pro James Blake when he was tackled to the ground by a NYPD undercover cop as he stood outside a mid-town Manhattan hotel in September 2015. He was quickly released, and NYPD Commissioner Bill Bratton and Mayor Bill DeBlasio publicly apologized to him.

It didn't answer the question why so many Black celebrities, professionals, business leaders, and even some state legislators and House representatives, and federal officials as was the case with Holder, and even Black cops out of uniform, are and can be hauled or slammed to the curb and arrested at any time no matter their status or appearance?

One answer is that well-to-do Blacks are more likely to live, work, seek entertainment, and travel in and through neighborhoods and locales that are far removed from inner city neighborhoods. They are likely to draw the attention of not only police, but also neighbors, residents, and business-persons in those areas. It takes only one phone call or a report to the police of suspicious activity and the fingering of that person as the suspect to warrant a stop. This invariably sets off an ugly encounter when he or she is stopped, patted down, verbally assailed or handcuffed by officers.

* * * * *

The other answer is the bedrock of well-known stereotypes that type Black men as violent, crime prone, drug peddlers, and inherently hostile to authority. Stereotypes are blanket negative depictions of an entire group regardless of the class or status of members of that group. So, a police officer who sees a Blake standing in front of a midtown Manhattan hotel waiting for a cab to go make a presentation to a corporate group may not regard him as someone of stature and importance. Rather he is someone to be accosted, no matter how vague, tenuous and mistaken an identification is made of criminal activity in the area.

There's yet another reason, that's whispered, mentioned only in hushed terms, and always hotly denied by authorities. And that it's the very prominence of the Blacks who are often subject to harassment as the cause of the profiling. The finger-point at this subtle and unstated bias came to a head in a 2013 study that found that Black NFL players were ten times more likely than white players to be stopped and arrested. Their arrest almost always came after traffic stops. The telling point was not the arrest, since in some of the cases the Black players had committed an offense, but the stops. In almost all cases they were driving expensive, late model cars. To some officers, this instantly tagged them as a possible drug dealer or engaged in some illicit activity. To others their apparent wealth may have stirred resentment against them.

Countless studies have repeatedly underscored the fact that Blacks are far more likely to be stopped, searched and arrested in nearly every category of crime than whites. That is irrespective of their status or prominence.

* * * * *

The one arena that has been one of the greatest finger points at the alleged proclivity of Black men to commit acts of misconduct has been just that the athletic sports arena. One case in particular typified this. In January 2013, Seattle Seahawks all-pro cornerback Richard Sherman exploded in a profanity laced diatribe to an interviewer on the sidelines after Seattle's NFL championship win over the San Francisco 49ers.

The predictable quickly happened with. The stereotypes flew fast and furious. Sherman was lambasted by sportswriters and broadcasters as a "thug," "dirtbag," scum," and "disgrace." Those were the genteel ones. The booing chorus heaped on him the racist favorites, "gorilla," "ape," "monkey," and "animal." The epithets were amply punctuated with the N-word.

Sherman quickly back pedaled from his tirade against the opposing player that stirred the rant. He bitingly recognized that he was not just a target for his supposedly loose brained, bad behavior in front of a TV camera, but had been instantly transformed into the nation's new walking, emblematic racial stereotype, "To use racial slurs and bullying language far worse than what you'll see from me. It's sad and somewhat unbelievable to me that the world is still this way." It was and the last person that should have been surprised at that was Sherman if he had paid even the least bit of attention to the unabashed and gleeful racial mugging in the past of the legion of bad behaving Black sports notables.

The prevalent thug image by many fans and observers of Black pro football players was not merely a matter of repugnant and jaded personal bias. It has had a troubling consequence. A study by *USA Today* in 2013 found marked differences in how authorities handled Black NFL players vs. white players during traffic stops. The overwhelming majority of the Black players were arrested for charges related to their driver's license. No white players were arrested for the same thing. Black players were pulled over for playing their music too loud. No white players were stopped for this. And white players were almost never arrested on charges after a search of their vehicle. A number of Black players were.

The racial trashing of Sherman was on the surface silly stuff. The arsenal of stereotypes and negative typecasting they were anchored in are not. Once these stereotype are planted, it's virtually impossible to root out.

Sherman was a near textbook example of this. His lofty academic accomplishments, Stanford University degree, and often thoughtful and entertaining interviews and literary analysis and comment on sports, and even at times, social issues, and tout of education for young Blacks meant absolutely nothing to the race baiters.

There was another predictable thing that was very much a part of the Sherman saga. That's denial. The instant that the race baiting flew hot and heavy at Sherman. There was a mighty effort made by some sportswriters to dismiss the attacks on Sherman as just the sick rants of a handful of racists who hid behind the relative anonymity of Twitter. The critics continued to place full blame on him for triggering such passionate and angered outbursts from so many people. The message was that the few times that race cropped up against him was unfortunate but had no real significance to explain the massive mostly negative public fascination with a few moments of a rant from a football player of all persons.

This was pretty much the same pattern with former San Francisco quarterback Colin Kaepernick. He became a *cause célèbre* in 2017 among many Blacks for his taking a knee on the sidelines before games during the playing of the national Anthem. The knee was the protest over police slayings of unarmed Blacks. He was also a *cause célèbre* among the NFL owners and tens of thousands of white fans and a number of sportswriters and broadcaster-jocks. They harangued, assailed, and vilified him. The NFL owners blackballed him from the league. Despite the lip service that some NFL owners gave to their support of freedom of expression, and their assurance that the NFL did not bar players from protesting racial injustices, the stern warning to the Black players who make up the bulk of NFL players, in Kap's blackballing, was loud and clear. You can protest racism and police shootings of Blacks. But you can't protest it in our League, on our playing field, and especially during the playing of the national anthem.

In the end, Sherman and Kaepernick found out that it didn't much matter how prominent, wealthy, or celebrated the Black is they too can be victimized by racial stereotypes. Sherman and Kaepernick did much to put their teams in

Super Bowls. That normally would have earned them acco-
lades as heroes for it that is until in the case of Sherman, his
rant, and Kaepernick's protest, again blew the hinge off the
door of racial stereotypes.

* * * * *

Sherman was not by any stretch the most celebrated
Black athlete to get the image mugging treatment following a
real or perceived misstep. That dubious honor went to perhaps
the world's most recognizable athlete, golfer Tiger Woods.
In 2004, *Vanity Fair* made it official when it made Tiger a
member in good standing in the echelon of gang banging,
drive by shooting, menacing, thug life, sexually on the make,
young Black males. At least that's what the lengthy pack of
Tiger bashers quickly branded the pumping iron, buffed,
ghetto trademark ski cap wearing Tiger that ungraced the
cover of *Vanity Fair.* They and a handful of Black commentators gloated that the magazine dumped on Tiger something
that he allegedly spent the better part of a decade fleeing in
horror from, namely his blackness.

The nonsensical talk of Calabanasian, as he coined his
mixed-race (Caucasian, black, Native American and Asian)
heritage, and his public duck and dodge of any identification
with Black causes, supposedly was final proof that Tiger had
danced down the O.J. Simpson path of scrupulous non-iden-
tification with Black causes. Whether true or not, the troubling fact was that he had been scorned, trashed, and battered
by many in the corporate and Golf World.

Any other time, the *Vanity Fair* shot would have been laughed away or shrugged off as just fun and games stuff. It would do little to change the universal perception of the carefully honed Wheaties Box, wholesome, image of the Golf World's reigning superstar. Indeed, when the photo was snapped in 2006, the devoted family man, clean Gene image of Tiger was still deeply frozen in the public's psyche. The parade of porn figures, lap dancers, cocktail waitresses, and call girls who allegedly wound up in Tiger's lair have rendered that image laughable, even pitiable. That made the *Vanity Fair* cover thug life looking Tiger totally believable.

Still, Tiger as racial martyr, closet thug, and America's new racial bad boy seemed ridiculous. The racial stereotypes that the *Vanity Fair*-Tiger shot reinforced, though, was not. It's the shortest of short steps to think that if a fallen from the perch Tiger could be depicted as a caricature of the terrifying image that much of the public still harbors about young Black males, then that image seemed real, even more terrifying, and the consequences were just as dangerous.

Tiger didn't commit any crime, and the only one that he hurt was his wife, family, sponsors, and the fantasy image of him as the Simon-pure sportsman. For that he paid a dear price with many sponsors who fled in droves from him and a wide swatch of the general public that no longer saw him as their fantasy golf idol. The *Vanity Fair* cover was just the capper.

CHAPTER 11

Politics, Race and the Clinton Crime Bill

Twenty-two years after then President Bill Clinton signed his 1994 Omnibus Crime Bill he was at a May 13 event in Patterson, New Jersey. The occasion was a campaign event for his wife, Democratic presidential contender, Hillary Clinton. During the question and answer period, an audience member asked Clinton, "Why did you put more people in prison?" This was in obvious reference to his crime bill. A visibly angered Clinton lost his cool for the moment and lashed back that the questioner was ignorant of the legislation. He cited the provision in the bill that exempted first-time drug offenders from the harsher drug sentencing laws. The questioner was promptly escorted out of the rally hall.

Clinton didn't stop there and went on to brag that the

$30 billion crime bill put an additional 100,000 police officers on the streets while tightening gun ownership rules. Clinton may have got his point across and some applause from the audience in the process and the questioner booted from the rally, but it didn't change some brutal realities about the crime bill.

The most immediate was its drag on Hillary's campaign. On more than one occasion during the campaign she had a Black Lives Matter member in her face lambasting her for giving nodding approval at the time to the crime bill. She was ripped repeatedly for the quip she made in a speech in 1996 in New Hampshire about the crime bill, "They are often connected to big drug cartels, they are not just gangs of kids anymore. They are often the kinds of kids that are called super-predators—no conscience, no empathy. We can talk about why they ended up that way, but first, we have to bring them to heel."

Clinton swore she meant no racial harm with this characterization of criminals, and even issued a statement, "Looking back, I shouldn't have used those words, and I wouldn't use them today." Many Blacks were having none of it. They blasted her for employing this term as a not-so-thinly veiled racist code term for Blacks. Clinton saw political danger here and time for some belated fence mending. So, whenever she got the chance during the campaign she did what could be called a *mea culpa* for hubby, Bill's still much talked about and much maligned crime bill. Her most memorable about-face was in a speech in Harlem in

February 2016 when she called for "end-to-end" criminal justice reform, more support for African-American home-owners and a hefty $20 billion boost to tackle Great Depression joblessness in poor and minority communities. She struck that theme and made the pledge again several more times on the campaign trail.

However, this did not silence the Hillary critics on the Left, nor many Blacks who backed Clinton, but still slapped a guilt by marital association accusation on her for the bill. The heat on Hillary was so intense over the bill and its dire consequences for Blacks that even Bill felt he had to do a slight back-peddle a couple of times during the campaign on the bill. In May 2015, he told an interviewer "The problem is the way it was written and implemented. We have too wide a net. We have too many people in prison. And we wound up spending - putting so many people in prison that there wasn't enough money left to educate them, train them for new jobs, and increase the chances when they came out that they could live productive lives." Clinton went a bit further and even praised his wife for her de facto renunciation of the draconian effects of the bill.

* * * * *

While the harsh bill was the brainchild of Presidents Ronald Reagan and Bush Sr., they could not have gotten it through a mostly Democratic-controlled Congress in the 1980s and early 1990s. But Clinton did. He muscled it through Congress. The bill shelled out the billions to the states and feds to hire more police and prosecutors build new prisons, and courts, and establish crime commissions.

It criminalized thousands, mostly Blacks and Latinos, for petty crimes and drug possession, ignited the biggest prison-police boom in U.S history, spurred dozens of states to adopt three strikes laws, led to the deadly rash of racial profiling cases, and widened the gaping racial disparities in prison sentencing. The anti-crime legislative mania also tacitly encouraged more states to disenfranchise thousands of ex-felons. The law added more than 30 new provisions for the death penalty in federal law. To no surprise, the majority of those that await execution are Black men. In 1993, there were less than a half million Blacks in America's jails. That figure soared to more than 2 million in 2018 with about half of them Black.

Hillary's public pledge during the campaign to change that took the battle against crime in the direction that it should have gone twenty years ago. And that was to put massive resources into investment and repair in poor and minority communities, while committing to fight to end the blatant racial disparities in arrests, sentencing, imprisonment, and the death penalty that have become the trademark of the criminal justice system. The suspicion, though, was that she made those promises only to appease her core back supporters, and only after repeated and withering slams by Black Lives Matter.

This ignored too much. It's true that incarceration is not and never has been the answer to the root cause of crime.

However, most Americans in the early 1990s were in no mood for sociological answers to crime. Polls showed that a majority of Americans were in near hysteria over the rising crime numbers, a soaring murder and drug use rate, and the urban riots following the Rodney King beating in 1991 and the acquittal of the LAPD officers in the beating in 1992. They clamored for a crackdown, and that included a significant number of Blacks who felt under siege from gangs and drugs.

By then, the old racial stereotypes of Black males as the poster boys for crime, violence, and lawlessness in America fed by Nixon and then the Reagan administration's get tough on crime in the inner-city policies and rhetoric and the nightly diet of news scenes of gory gang and drive by shootings in Black neighborhoods ensured that those stereotypes become even more firmly entrenched in the public mind.

*　*　*　*　*

The fear of Black crime was so great that even a majority of the Congressional Black Caucus members voted for the bill mostly in response to demands from their terrified constituents about raging crime. Some, like the Clintons, have in the decades since the bill's passage regretted their vote, and have sharply criticized the harsh crime approach then. But they, like Bill and many others, have had two decades to see the racially corrosive effects of the bill. Crime was simply no longer the politically expedient tough on crime issue and the issue to pander to the public and voters that it was for politicians then. It had been replaced by the greater fear of terrorism.

So, it wasn't necessary for Hillary to admit shame and guilt over a law passed two decades before her presidential run that much of the public wanted and drew broad bi-partisan support from Democrats, including many Black Democrats. If Hillary backed the bill then, it was because a majority of Americans also backed it. To knock her for not being divinely oracular about the terrible downsides of the bill, defied logic, common sense, and history.

The challenge then was not to hold Hillary's feet to the fire for a policy from the past that's had and has bad consequences for the present. But to hold her feet to the flame to deliver on her pledge to push for meaningful criminal justice system reforms, and programs and initiatives to aid the urban poor if she ever got in the White House. The Omnibus Crime Bill is, and forever, would remain part of Bill's legacy, the good, and the much larger bad of it. The problem is that the bad of it grew out of and pandered to the basest fears and hysteria, and stereotypes, of Blacks as the America's perennial menace to society.

Given the heightened awareness and sensitivity, to the colossal damage and long history of racially tagging Black youth as inherently violent, the anger over this, and the damage wreaked by the crime bill almost certainly cost Clinton more than a few Black votes. Those votes may in the end have done much to cost her the White House. In a perverse, and ironic way, thus proving that racial stereotypes can take a heavy toll on more than just Blacks.

CHAPTER 12

The Drug War in Black and White

O n March 29, 2017, the mood at the White House was somber when Trump signed an executive order establishing a commission charged with making recommendations on dealing with the Opioid crisis. At the signing, all the talk by Trump and other administration officials was about a big ramp up in treatment, counseling, addiction recovery programs, and health services to alleviate the crisis. They, and the media, coined the term, "epidemic." This suggested that it was an illness, a sickness, a condition, but not a criminal offense. There was not one word from Trump or White House officials at the signing about more arrests, tougher sentencing, and incarceration for offenders.

Trump appointed his close political backer, then New Jersey Governor Chris Christie to head up the commission

that would come back with the recommendations on dealing with the crisis. Christie made plain what the focus would
be on, "What we need to come to grips with is addiction is a
disease and no life is disposable. We can help people by giving
them appropriate treatment."

The compassion, sympathy, and official search to find
ways to help white Opioid addicts that oozed out the White
House that day was in sharp contrast to the memo Attorney
General Jeff Sessions issued a few weeks later. Sessions ordered U.S. attorneys around the country to get tough on drug
crimes by demanding more convictions and jail time. Sessions wasn't talking about white addicts, the ones whom the
Opioid crisis affected the most.

There were three reasons for that. One is politics. The
Opioid crisis slammed suburban and rural areas, big sections
of whom were Trump voter friendly. The second was that it
had become a serious health issue with reports that there were
more than a million hospitalizations in 2016 from Opioid addiction. The third was race. Countless studies showed that
Blacks use drugs about the same as whites, some drugs such
as marijuana, and powdered cocaine even less. Yet, for three
decades, since the 1980s, they were the ones slapped with
massive arrests, mandatory minimum sentences, and lengthy
prison terms. They were the ones who packed America's jails
and prisons for drug crimes. They were the ones who would
again be prime targets when Attorney General Jeff Sessions
reignited the drug war.

Whether it was cocaine, marijuana, or the heroin surge

in the rural areas and the suburbs, the relatively few times that whites were popped for drug use, the pipeline for them was never to the courts and jails, but to counseling and treatment, therapy, and prayers. Their drug abuse was chalked up to escape, frustration, or restless youthful experimenting. They got heart wringing indulgent sympathy, compassion, and a never-ending soul search for rational explanations, or should I say justification, for their acts that were deemed crimes when the offenders are Black.

* * * * *

Black drug users also lacked something else that white rural and suburban drug users didn't. That was political clout. The instant heroin became a "crisis" among whites, and now Opioid an "epidemic," arch GOP conservative congresspersons in whose districts the "crisis" and "epidemic" hit leaped over themselves to declare the problem a health problem. They proposed a string of new initiatives to treat the problem as a health problem. Police officials quickly followed suit. Dozens of police departments publicly invited heroin users who wanted help to stop in their local police headquarters even in many cases with drugs and needles in or on their person. They would not be arrested but shuttled promptly to a treatment program; no questions asked.

There was one final great cruelty in the glaring racial double standard on drugs. The reports and stats on Opioid and heroin addition, the wrath of news stories and features on it, and the calls for legislative action to deal with the problem, did not change the deeply embedded perception that drugs in America invariably comes with a young, Black face. Trump's call for compassion and treatment for Opioid addicts wouldn't change that.

* * * * *

Sessions made it official when he announced in May 2017 that the federal government would reboot its war on drugs. The official word came down in the form of memos from Sessions that ordered federal prosecutors to cease and desist on the soft approach former Attorney General Eric Holder took toward prosecuting petty drug offenders. Now prosecutors would demand the harshest sentence, must use the threat to harshly pile on sentence enhancements to browbeat drug offenders into copping a guilty plea. They would also be required to itemize the drugs an offender uses to insure they are slapped with the minimum mandatory sentence.

Sessions wasn't talking about cracking down on the use of the hard stuff. only He had a near paranoid obsession with pot. He railed against its use, and called it one of the worst drug evils, and is convinced it is undermining the nation's morals. Sessions long chomped at the bit to cop the title as America's number one drug warrior. He took giddy delight as a federal prosecutor and a U.S. Attorney in Alabama in putting the hammer to drug offenders whenever he could. Sessions would have likely scoffed at the frank admission by disgraced Nixon White House advisor John Ehrlichman, in an interview in Harpers in 1994, that the war on drugs was not about law enforcement getting a handle on drug sales and use, but another weapon to lock up as many Blacks as possible.

From its inception in the 1970s, the war on drugs was a ruthless, relentless, and naked war on minorities, especially African-Americans. Former President Obama and Eric Holder got that. They made it clear that it was time to rethink how the war was being fought and who its main casualties have been. They pushed hard to get Congress to wipe out a good deal of the blatantly racially skewed harsh drug sentencing for crack versus powder cocaine possession and to eliminate minimum mandatory sentencing. Congress didn't finish the job and as long as Sessions was in the driver's seat at the Justice Department it wouldn't. The Obama and Holder reforms in low level drug prosecutions did produce positive and dramatic results. The number of minimum mandatory sentences imposed plunged, and there was much more reliance on drug counseling and diversion programs for petty offenders.

You could kiss that good-by with Sessions. Even though countless surveys have found that whites and Blacks use drugs in about the same rate, more than 70 percent of those prosecuted in federal courts for drug possession and sale (mostly small amounts of crack cocaine) and given stiff mandatory sentences were Blacks. Most of those who deal and use crack cocaine aren't violent prone gang members, but poor, and increasingly female, young Blacks. They clearly needed treatment not long prison stretches but treatment and rehabilitation options too. Obama and Holder understood that.

* * * * *

The fed war on drugs before Obama and Holder, and reignited under Sessions, targeted Blacks for a good reason. The top-heavy drug use by young whites—and the crime and violence that go with it—has never stirred any public outcry for mass arrests, prosecutions, and tough prison sentences for white drug dealers, many of whom deal drugs that are directly linked to serious crime and violence. Whites unlucky enough to get popped for drug possession are treated with compassion, prayer sessions, expensive psychiatric counseling, treatment and rehab programs, and drug diversion programs.

A frank admission that the laws are biased and unfair and have not done much to combat the drug plague, would be an admission of failure. It would ignite a real soul-searching over whether all the billions of dollars that have been squandered in the failed and flawed drug war—the lives ruined by it, and the families torn apart by the rigid and unequal enforcement of the laws—has really accomplished anything.

This might call into question why people use and abuse drugs in the first place—and if it is really the government's business to turn the legal screws on some drug users while turning a blind eye to others?

The greatest fallout from the nation's failed drug policy is that it had further embedded the widespread notion that the drug problem is exclusively a Black problem. This made it easy for on-the-make politicians to grab votes, garner press attention, and balloon state prison budgets to jail more Black offenders, while continuing to feed the illusion that we are winning the drug war.

This meant little to Sessions. In his fundamentalist, self-righteous, puritanical world, drug users were the scourge of the nation. They must be swiftly and mercilessly removed from the streets, workplaces, schools, and any other place that their presence subverts the good upstanding morals of the nation. Sessions said as much in a memo when he claimed that his tough drug crackdown would "advance public safety and promote respect for our legal system." It would do neither. It would continue to balloon prison building, the hiring and maintaining of waves of corrections officers, and further bloat state budgets. Worst of all it would again do what it was always intended to do and that's be a war on minorities and especially Blacks.

CHAPTER 13

The Revolving Prison Door

apper Meek Mill did more than rouse the anger of former San Francisco 49ers quarterback Colin Kaepernick and Rap Mogul Jay-Z in November 2017. Both loudly spoke out against Mill being plopped back in prison for a probation violation. There was even disgust from another unexpected source to Mill's probation bust. New England Patriots owner Robert Kraft after an April 2018 visit to Mill in jail said that his incarceration, "Makes it clear to me we have to do something with criminal justice reform. His kind of case, to be in a situation like this, it's really bad."

Though Mill was released shortly afterwards, the outrage from sports and music world notables didn't change the fact that he was behind the bars for a very questionable probation violation. His presence in jail again cast the strong glare back

on a part of the criminal justice system that has been too often ignored, overlooked or not even seen. That's the blatantly
racially biased probation and parole system.

Mill's defenders pointed the damning finger at the seeming injustice of his being slapped back in prison for a long
stretch for relatively minor parole violations by what they call
a biased female judge with an ax to grind against him. The
he said, she said debate over what he or she did to wind up
behind bars was not the real issue. The issue is that before he
was sent back to prison he was one of millions of Black men
who were under the iron thumb of the parole system.

The racial disparities between Blacks and whites on parole are staggering. Blacks make up more than 40 percent of
all parolees in the country. In some states, the percent and
number of Blacks on parole is far higher. They are more likely
to be on parole than whites and stay on parole for a longer
time. This is where the Mill case and the plight of other black
parolees are a crisis issue. They are far more likely than whites
to be plopped back in prison for violations. The violations are
often arbitrary, voluminous, and can be petty. The loud message that parole sends is that the parolee is completely under
the control of a parole officer or agency, and his every action
is being closely watched and monitored.

The upside for defenders of a tight, overbearing parole
system is that this is the best way to ensure that ex-felons,
especially violent ex-felons do not commit crimes again and
menace society. This part makes sense. What doesn't is that
a huge number of those on parole are not violent offenders,

career criminals, or pose a recidivist threat. They are low level drug offenders or were convicted of petty crimes. Studies have repeatedly shown that providing these individuals with job training and drug counseling programs are a far more cost-effective way to insure they do not repeat their crimes.

Then there is the widespread notion that parolees are sent back to prison because they have committed new crimes. This is not true. A parolee is more likely to be returned to prison for any number of technical violations of their parole, which could include something as seemingly petty as being late for or missing appointments with the parole officer. In Mill's case, the violations cited were a dispute with a fan, and a dispute over a motorbike on a street during a music video shoot. The decision to send Mill back was made by a judge. However, in most cases the decision to shuttle a parolee back to prison is made by a supervising parole officer and that decision can be at the whim of the officer.

*   *   *   *   *

There's yet another danger with the parole system. With crime down, and more felons being released back to the streets, the pressure is great to make sure that these felons are even more tightly controlled. Public fears over ex-felons running amok with no one watching the store, is fed by sensationalist headlines of rapes and multiple shootings by violent ex-felons. This in turn has a spiraling effect. The public demands tighter controls and scrutiny on parolees, and parole officers comply by further tightening the reins on them. Black men on parole are watched even closer. This makes it even harder for many to find a decent job, provide for their family, and return to anything that remotely resembles normalcy in their lives. The result is predictable. These men are front line candidates for a return to a prison cell.

The parole back to-prison pipeline has wreaked massive social and political havoc on families and communities. It has been a factor in the bloat in federal and state spending on prison construction, maintenance, and the escalation in the number of prosecutors needed to handle the continuing flood of criminal cases.

The stock reason for criminalizing a huge segment of a generation of young Blacks is that they are crime-prone and lack family values. However, reports and studies by the Justice Department, the U.S. Sentencing Commission, as well as universities and foundations confirm that broken homes and bad genes have little to do with crime rates. High joblessness, failing public schools, budget cutbacks in skills training and placement programs, the refusal of employers to hire those with criminal records, and the gaping racial disparity in the drug sentencing laws are the major reasons why far more Blacks than whites are behind bars.

The hard tie between joblessness, racism, and re-imprisonment was brought into dramatic focus in a series of studies in 2006 and 2007 by then University of Wisconsin graduate researcher Devah Pager. She found that Black men without a criminal record were less likely to find a job than white men with criminal records.

Pager's finger-point at discrimination as the main reason for the racial disparity in hiring set off howls of protest from employers, trade groups and even a Nobel Prize winner. They lambasted her for faulty research. Her sample was much too small, they said, and the questions too vague. They pointed to the ocean of state and federal laws that ban racial discrimination. But then she duplicated her study. She surveyed nearly 1,500 private employers in New York City.

She used teams of Black and white testers, standardized resumes, and she followed up their visits with telephone interviews with employers. These are the standard methods researchers use to test racial discrimination. The results were exactly the same as in her earlier study, despite the fact that New York has some of the nation's toughest laws against job discrimination. Whites with no degrees, and even criminal records, were hired in many instances before Blacks with college degrees.

*   *   *   *   *

Countless other research studies, the Urban League's annual State of Black America reports, and the numerous discrimination complaints reviewed by the Equal Employment Opportunity Commission yearly reveal that employers have devised endless dodges to evade anti-discrimination laws. That includes rejecting applicants by their names or areas of the city they live in. Black applicants may be incorrectly told that jobs advertised were filled already.

In one infamous seven-month comprehensive

university study of the hiring practices of hundreds of Chicago area employers back in 2000, many top company officials when interviewed said they would not hire Blacks. When asked to assess the work ethic of white, Black and Latino employees by race, nearly 40 percent of the employer's ranked blacks dead last.

The employers routinely described Blacks as being "unskilled," "uneducated," "illiterate," "dishonest," "lacking initiative," "involved with gangs and drugs" or "unstable," of having "no family values" and being "poor role models." The consensus among these employers was that Blacks brought their alleged pathologies to the work place and were to be avoided at all costs. Not only white employers expressed such views; researchers found that Black business owners shared many of the same negative attitudes. The pattern of erecting endless dodges to not hire Blacks has not abated in the years since the Chicago study and Pager's research studies. A report from the University of Illinois at Chicago's Great Cities Institute in 2016 found that nearly half of young Black males aged 20-24 were jobless in Chicago.

So, when an African-American male or female who has been recently released from prison shows up at a personnel office seeking a job that has been advertised as open, and that person is not hired it's a safe bet that the cause for rejection is not just his or her inadequate qualifications that puts a rejection slip in their hand, but race; with the added burden of a prison record. This last point can't be stressed enough. One study even found that even Blacks without a criminal record were nearly three times as likely to get a callback from employers as Blacks with a criminal record.

Mill was simply a high-profile example, but example nonetheless, of a Black that got no break from a judge who used the parole system to put him back in a cell for an alleged violation. The figures amply show that a broken parole system has put many more like him back in jail cells. The only consolation in his case is that because of his celebrity he cast an intense spotlight on this.

CHAPTER 14

The Vile Fascination with the Monkey Image of the Obamas (and African-Americans)

The CEO of the Tennessee Hospitality Association, Walt Baker, made brief news in March 2010. His silly, sick, demeaning depiction of then First Lady Michelle Obama as a chimp went viral. However, what raised eyebrows even more was not the grotesque depiction of Michelle. It was Baker's clueless defense. The instant the storm broke, Nashville's mayor and the state's GOP leaders denounced him, and the contract for his marketing firm, Mercatus Communications, to help promote the city's new convention center was summarily yanked. In response, Baker predictably wailed that he was not a bigot or racially insensitive, and that the cartoon was nothing but political humor.

He fervently believed that. He just as fervently believed that lampooning Michelle Obama and then President Obama as a monkey, ape, or gorilla was just fun and games. He and the pack of race baiting websites, chat rooms, college frat parties, and student websites that non-stop ridiculed the Obamas (and African-Americans) during virtually every moment of their White House tenure in assorted offbeat, crude, vile cartoons and always with the vile depiction as monkeys or apes was by now standard fare. It's no accident that it is.

The long, sordid and savage history of racist stereotyping of African-Americans has been the stock in trade of race baiting and racial ridicule for more than century. A few grotesque book titles from a century ago, such as *The Negro a Beast, The Negro, a Menace to American Civilization*, and *The Clansman* depicted blacks as apes, monkeys, bestial, and animal like. The image stuck in books, magazines, journals, and deeply colored the thinking of many Americans of that day... that day?

In the movie version of Rudyard Kipling children's classic, *The Jungle Book*, the Disney Studios in 1967 graduated from the other standard animal depiction of African-Americans as black crows to depicting African-Americans as the monkey like jive, gibberish blathering King Louie. The film was remade in 1994.

Fifteen years later in 2009, *New York Post* Cartoonist Sean Delonas ignited a firestorm with his casual depiction of Obama as a monkey. He did it precisely because that image didn't die a century, half century, a decade, or at any point in time. In 2007 Penn State researchers conducted six separate studies and found that many Americans still linked Blacks with apes and monkeys. Many of the participants in the survey were young and had absolutely no knowledge of the vicious stereotyping of Blacks of years past. Their findings with the provocative title "Not Yet Human: Implicit Knowledge, Historical Dehumanization and Contemporary Consequences," in the February 2008 issue of *Journal of Personality and Social Psychology*, was conducted by the American Psychological Association.

The majority of the participants in the studies bristled at the faintest hint that they had any racial bias. Yet, the animal savagery image and Blacks was very much on their minds. The researchers found that participants—and that included even those with no stated prejudices or knowledge of the historical images—were quicker to associate Blacks with apes than they were to associate whites with apes.

* * * * *

The pillorying of the Obama's with the monkey and ape depiction took and even more odious and bizarre turn in April 2011 when Orange County, California. GOP Central Committee member Marilyn Davenport blasted out an email depicting not only Obama, but his entire family as monkeys. Again, it was sick, vile, and disgusting. However, that was not the worst part of it. Even her witless defense of the photo as just a "joke," was not the worst part of her slur. The worst part was the reaction of GOP officials.

The local party chair, Scott Baugh, appropriately blasted the email, saying it "drips with racism," and said Davenport should resign. He claimed that the bylaws prevented him from expelling Davenport. But he did not call for a change in the bylaws to make expulsion possible, or even indicate when or if he would move to censure Davenport. To their credit, some former GOP state officials did call for her expulsion. No immediate action of any kind was taken against Davenport.

The non-action paled in comparison to the reaction of other GOP officials who either downplayed it as "much ado about nothing," as Davenport branded it, or defended her. Davenport was not some raving Tea Party haranguer. She was a member in good standing of the powerful and well-connected Orange County GOP party machine. In Democrat-leaning California, this was not insignificant. Orange County was still one of the reddest counties in Southern California, and a traditional bastion of GOP conservatism. The Orange County Republican Party could still muster tens of thousands of votes for local, state, congressional and presidential candidates. Republican presidential candidates have beat a steady path to the county for decades to secure votes and money. That included Trump on one of his rare forays to California.

Davenport, for her part, adamantly said she wouldn't resign. She wouldn't have dug her heels in on staying at her party post if she wasn't confident that she had the backing of more than a few party members.

* * * * *

Those GOP Davenport cheerleaders weren't just in Orange County. Other party officials essentially blew off the controversy as a non-issue. This spoke to the GOP's continual denial and subtle or flat-out stoke of the racial fires.

Davenport underlined her despicable depiction of Obama with the caption, "Now you know why there's no birth certificate." That was just the crude version of what Trump had been parroting in his crusade to bait Obama on his birth certificate.

That worked because polls consistently showed that a significant minority, possibly a majority, of the GOP rank-and-file clung to the false belief that Obama was a fake American citizen. Trump would not have gotten to first base with his birth certificate ploy if these millions didn't give credence to it. The controversy had enough juice to draw Obama at one point into it when, in an interview in April 2011, he made more than a veiled reference to it when he said, "We're not really worrying about conspiracy theories or birth certificates."

Davenport's slanderous email depiction of Obama and family, her refusal to see anything wrong with it, and the foot-drag by GOP local and state officials in California and nationally to say or do anything about it at the time, spoke volumes about the GOP. During the 2012 presidential campaign, GOP presidential candidates, with the exception of Trump, disavowed the birther movement. And in the 2016 presidential campaign so did Trump. However, the record stood then that no top GOP party official ever censored, or publicly reprimanded, Davenport, or any of the throngs of Tea Party backers who paraded around signs that caricatured Obama and Michelle as apes and monkeys, or the chimp dolls that popped up on the 2008 campaign trail. That record of no reproach by the GOP for that still stands.

*   *   *   *   *

The monkey and ape depiction of the Obamas was not simply a case of take-no-prisoner partisan politics being politics or a dry academic exercise. The animal association and Blacks has had devastating real-life consequences. In hundreds of news stories from 1979 to 1999 the *Philadelphia Inquirer* was much more likely to describe African Americans than whites convicted of capital crimes with ape-relevant language, such as "barbaric," "beast," "brute," "savage" and "wild." Jurors in criminal cases were far more likely to judge Blacks more harshly than whites, and regard them and their crimes as savage, bestial, and heinous, and slap them with tougher sentences than whites.

Former First Lady Michelle Obama is a woman, a Black woman, and was a soft target for the frustrations and even scorn of the Obama loathers. During the campaign Obama opponents eagerly latched onto out-of-context statement she made at a campaign rally in which she allegedly questioned her faith in America and made a supposedly less than reverential reference to the flag. They brutally tarred her as a closet anti-American, race-obsessed, Black radical. That made her

an instant campaign liability. For weeks she virtually disappeared from the campaign trail during their initial run for
the White House in 2008.

She played a relatively low-key role in the White House
and succeeded in pretty much staying out of harm's way from
the hits of hubby Obama's avowed enemies. That is all except
when it came to the image assault from the eternal animal
mockery of Blacks, an image that Baker and multitudes of others see nothing wrong with. It's been that way for a century.

*   *   *   *   *

If the former president and First Lady couldn't escape
from the animal image that has been routinely used to depict
Blacks for generations, then there was no chance that Blacks
who were not the occupants of the Oval Office could escape
that vile characterization. The clothing manufacturer/retailer,
H&M found out just how sensitive the issue of making any
reference to monkeys and Blacks is when it ignited a firestorm
of protest for using a Black child to model a sweatshirt with a
"coolest monkey in the jungle" slogan. H&M quickly apologized for its *faux pas,* and the sweatshirt designer did a public
mea culpa for it, and pulled the ad from its website. However, H&M did not pull the sweatshirt from its product line.
It didn't miss a beat and continued to sell it online. The subtle
message was that whether it was trying to sell a sweatshirt,
or maligning a President and his wife and family, the ancient
totally racist, and totally dehumanizing, image of Blacks as
animals wouldn't die a quiet death.

CHAPTER 15

Would Stephon Clark be Different?

I n March 2018, prosecutors in Baton Rouge, Louisiana announced that the officers who gunned down Alton Sterling would not be prosecuted. The general reaction was ho hum, what else is new. The public cynicism over prosecuting cops who overuse deadly force against unarmed Blacks was well warranted. The list of names—Tamir Rice, Ezell Ford, Eric Garner, Michael Brown—who in the past few years have been the victims of police violence, are well-known. In every case, prosecutors have refused to file charges against any of the officers involved in their deaths.

The stock reasons were that there were no credible tapes, eyewitness testimony, or reports that prove the officers acted recklessly, the victims resisted arrest, or that the officers legitimately feared for their life. So, given the all-pervasive power of racial typecasting of young Black males, and the dismal scorecard for bringing charges against officers who gun them down, let alone getting a conviction against them, was there any real hope of beating the odds and getting and winning some prosecutions against offices who blatantly kill?

The tormenting question was what would change that? There was one case that seemed to show promise. That case was the killing of Stephon Clark in March 2017 by Sacramento police officers. At first glance, it seemed to have a better than even chance of beating the odds. Clark was unarmed. He was shot in his grandmother's backyard. The officers did not have their body cams on, apparently in violation of department policy. The chatter on the audio of the shooting was ordered muffled—again, in apparent violation of department policy.

Sacramento's Police Chief and Mayor publicly raised questions about the shooting. They took the unprecedented step of asking California Attorney General Xavier Becerra to have a hand in the investigation of the slaying. This was an obvious effort to head off the loud criticism that local DAs work hand in glove with local police and only in the rarest of rare cases will bring charges against officers who kill, no matter how blatant and outrageous the circumstances.

These were all pluses that gave some hope that the Clark case would be different. But they didn't cancel out the still towering obstacles to bring charges against cops who kill. One, was the words uttered by nearly every officer in every slaying of an unarmed civilian, "I feared for my life or the life of others."

* * * * *

These words are codified in law in many states. With only slight variations in the states the words are that an officer can use deadly force when he or she reasonably believes it's necessary to protect life. The operative words are "reasonably believes." Translated, that means that there is no written code, rule, or guideline for what exactly reasonable belief is or means. It's purely a judgment call by the officer the moment he or she draws his or her pistol and opens fire. The litany of "reasonable beliefs" can fill up a small phone book.

The suspect was reaching for a knife, gun, toothpick, holding a cell phone, tugging at his waistband, had his hands in his pocket, there was sudden movement of his vehicle. In the case of Clark, their defense would be that in the dark the cell phone that Clark had appeared to be a gun. And, since they were in chase, after a call of car break-ins in the area, they had reason to assume that Clark might have been armed.

If this sounded like a virtual license to kill, it is. And this almost certainly would be the way the Sacramento officers would play it to ensure that they would never hauled into a court docket. The bitter reality is that there is no ironclad standard of what is or isn't acceptable use of force. It almost always comes down to a judgment call by the officer. In the Rodney King beating case in 1992 in which four LAPD officers stood trial, defense attorneys turned the tables and painted King as the aggressor and claimed that the level of force used against him was justified.

The two New York City cases involving the killing cops of unarmed African immigrant, Amadou Diallo in 1999, and unarmed Sean Bell in 2006, the cops were tried but were acquitted. In each case, they claimed that they feared for their lives. The jury believed them and acquitted them.

The other obstacle to charging the Sacramento officers was the public. Surveys that measured overall confidence in police, have found the police topped out among the three highest-rated institutions out of 17 tested in terms of whites' confidence, behind only the military and small business. They are the ones who make up the majority on juries that inevitably hear the rare cases against police officers charged with the overuse of deadly force.

Despite overwhelming evidence that police do profile minorities, lie, cheat, and even commit crimes, jurors still are far more likely to believe the testimony of police and prosecution witnesses than witnesses, defendants, or even the victims, especially minority victims.

* * * * *

Prosecutors over the years have had many chances to bring charges against officers who have killed unarmed suspects. They haven't not solely because of their wanton pro-police bias. But because as long as officers have the near impregnable shield of being able to say "I feared for my life" when confronting victims such as Clark, it's near impossible to prosecute them.

However, it's not a completely impossible task.

Prosecutors have won convictions in a handful of police use of force cases. One of the best examples was the federal prosecution of the officers who beat Rodney King and were acquitted in state court in 1992. The prosecutors were aggressive, were scrupulous in their jury picks, carefully presented the evidence that the officers violated King's rights, and importantly did not rely solely on the videotape of the beating to make their case. Prosecutors that have won convictions of other cops who have killed unarmed Blacks have been just as aggressive, and thorough in presenting evidence and witness testimony. An important key in these rare cases and victories in police misconduct cases is that they were able to humanize the victims; meaning that they presented them as fathers and family men, or just plain innocents.

That, in effect, neutralized the negative racial stereotypes and the play on those stereotypes by defense attorneys for the officers. The result: They won convictions. The proliferation of cell phones and video cams, and officer use of body cams and dash cams increased the chance that with an officer who wantonly kills at least there's some visual documentation that can be presented as a counter to the stacked deck resources that an officer on trial in a misconduct case can draw on to win acquittal. Given the way videos in cop trials have been maligned and dismissed, it wouldn't guarantee a conviction but they are a powerful reminder that police are being scrutinized.

The Clark slaying would be a severe test of whether the system can be made to work on occasion for men such as him. There would be a lot of eyes watching.

CHAPTER 16

Obama's White House Didn't Bury Racial Stereotyping

There was still much talk about how Obama's White House win in 2008 demolished negative stereotypes about Blacks. That was always wishful thinking. A study by a team of researchers from several top universities the year he won election showed that stereotypes about poverty and crime remained just as frozen in time. The study found that much of the public still perceived that those most likely to commit crimes were poor, jobless, and Black. The surprise was that the negative racial stereotypes also applied to anyone, no matter their color, who was poor and jobless. If for instance a white committed a crime, the odds are that the respondents will reclassify that person as Black.

The jumbled mental contortions that many would go through to dub a white person Black solely based on their income and whether they were jailed didn't end there. If a person who was perceived as white was jailed, that person was still perceived to be Black even after their release. The study did more than affirm that race and poverty and crime are firmly rammed together in the public mind. It also showed that once the stereotype is planted, it's virtually impossible to root out. That was hardly new either.

In December 2017, one year after Trump won the White House the Washington Post exploded the notion that he won because he tapped into the anxiety and anger of many younger white workers over the loss of jobs and concern that the Democrats were the cause of that loss. The survey found that most of them that backed Trump weren't collecting an unemployment or welfare check and had been unceremoniously dumped from a plant or manufacturing outlet that fled to Taiwan, Mexico, or India. The issue was race, more particularly, their fear of, and hostility toward Blacks.

Trump knew this and consciously massaged, pandered, and stoked that racial hostility with his endless digs, attacks, and bashes on the campaign trail of immigrants and minorities. There were several other studies around the same time that found the same thing. That was that the more racially fearful and biased a person was the more likely they were to vote for and cheer Trump. Another study that measured racial bias and Trump backing was even more explicit and frightening. it found that the stronger a person's identification was as "white" and were told that they'd be outnumbered by non-whites in a few decades they were likely to back Trump. It went on and on, whites that liked Trump didn't like the idea of living next to Blacks, thought that Blacks lacked initiative, and were scared stiff of them as criminal predators. There was one final horrific point about Trump and racial bigotry.

The 2016 presidential election marked a high-water point in recent presidential elections in which race and racism played such a dominant part in putting a presidential contender in the White House. It featured a contender that by any standard was the last qualified presidential contender to come down the pike in decades. The great fear was that Trump's overt pander to the basest of racist fears worked so masterfully that it could be duplicated again and again in future elections.

* * * * *

Ther were two more troubling implications from these studies. One was that Obama's victory was more a personal triumph for him. It did not radically remap racial perceptions, let alone put an end to racial stereotyping. A significant percent of whites voted for him and were passionate about him because they were fed up with his predecessor George W. Bush's policies and believed that he would reverse those policies. The vote for him was race neutral. His victory was a tribute to his personal political organization and savvy as well as public fear and frustration about Bush.

The second implication was even more troubling. If

much of the public still viewed crime and poverty through narrow racial lens, and saw Trump as their antidote to that, then that would continue to stir public clamor for lawmakers, police and prosecutors to clean the streets of violent criminals, who are almost always seen as African-Americans. This could mean even more gang sweeps, court injunctions, stiff adult prison terms, three strikes laws, and incarceration for teens, the holding of accused teens indefinitely in juvenile jail detention. This was pretty much what Trump's election, rhetoric, and appointee promised to ensure.

Ironically, Obama inadvertently fed the negative perceptions of Blacks. In several much-publicized talks on the Black family, he blasted Black men for being missing in action from the home and shirking their family responsibility. It was a well-meaning effort to call attention to the chronic problems of Black males and families, but it also gave the impression that they are dysfunctional. It was a short step from that to conclude that these same men are more likely to be involved in crime than whites.

Obama's win was a two-edged sword. It was as billed a profound historic win. However, it also fanned the illusion that racial stereotypes were dead. In addition, it stirred an angry white backlash that put an ill-equipped, brash, self-serving bigot in the Oval Office. That was a steep price to pay to validate racial fearmongering.

What Can be Done

In 2006, the film, *Crash,* won the Academy Award for best picture because it forced Blacks as well as whites to honestly confront their stereotypes. The film set the course from the start when it opted to parody "racial correctness." The opening shot had two young Blacks charging out of a restaurant steaming mad. One of them claimed that a waitress ignored them, then gave them lousy service, and the whites in the restaurant gave them hostile stares solely because they were Black.

Then a white couple passes them on the street, and the wife locks arms with her husband for fear the two men would mug them. In an angry tirade, the angered young Black covers the wide gamut of myths, stereotypes, and negative perceptions that whites supposedly have of Blacks.

While Crash pierced and poked fun at racial stereotypes, a comprehensive Harvard University opinion poll in

2002 found that the racial attitudes of many whites about Blacks were snuggly wrapped in stereotypes. The majority of whites were probably genuinely convinced that America was a color-blind society, and that equal opportunity was a reality. They repeatedly told the Harvard pollsters that they believed Blacks and whites had attained social and economic equality. Similar results have been found in other polls in the years since the that surveyed racial attitudes.

If many whites thought racial equality was a reality, that was more proof to many Blacks that whites were in deliberate racial denial. But many whites didn't claim Blacks were treated equally simply to mask their racial hostility to Blacks. They no longer saw "Whites only" signs and redneck Southern cops unleashing police dogs, turning fire hoses on and beating hapless Black demonstrators. Whites turned on their TVs and saw numerous Black newscasters and talk show hosts, topped by TV's richest and most popular celebrity, Oprah Winfrey.

They saw mega-rich black entertainers and athletes pampered and fawned over by a doting media and an adoring public. They saw TV commercials that pictured Blacks living in trendy integrated suburban homes, sending their kids to integrated schools and driving expensive cars. They saw Blacks in high-profile policy-making positions in first, the Bush administration from 2001-2009. Then followed by the election of the nation's first African-American president, which millions of whites voted for. They saw dozens of Blacks in Congress, many more in state legislatures and city halls. They saw Blacks heading corporations and universities.

* * * * *

However, this didn't change the deepest part of America's racial fault which has always been and still remain America's chronic racial divide. This has spawned the pack of vile but durable racial stereotypes, fears, and antagonisms. Black males have been the special target of negative typecasting. They've routinely been depicted as crime prone, derelict, sexual menaces and chronic underachievers. University researchers found that Obama's win didn't appreciably change these stereotypes. Prominent, wealthy, high achieving Blacks have gotten no pass from the stereotypes, and that included Obama and former Attorney General Holder. Both repeatedly cited painful instances of racial slights, harassment, abuse, and a litany of wrong headed cracks, digs, and perceptions about them.

If many police, storekeepers, public officials, and just the average Joe and Jane on the streets, have a vague or deep-seated notion of Blacks as crime prone, drug peddlers, and inherently hostile to authority, then it takes little imagination to know that that negative perception can easily be transferred to even a Black who is nattily dressed, carrying a laptop, or briefcase, and driving a late model car. Stereotypes are blanket negative depictions of an entire group regardless of the class or status of members of that group.

So, it's no stretch to see how the police officer who saw noted Black tennis pro James Blake standing in front of a midtown Manhattan hotel waiting for a cab to go make a presentation to a corporate group would not see him as a respected and recognizable professional athlete but someone who is a prime criminal suspect. And then when the mistake is recognized extend no immediate apology, but loud and long defense for his actions.

If a Blake could be body-slammed to the ground, cuffed, and had a gun drawn on him in broad daylight on a busy Manhattan street, then the fate of poor Blacks without Blake's celebrity is even more tenuous. That was exactly the case when in the space of a few days in 2016 that Baltimore Police Lieutenant Brian Rice was scheduled for trial in the death of Freddie Gray, the Justice Department announced that it would not conduct a probe into the police shooting of Alton Sterling in Baton Rouge, La., nor one in the shooting of Philando Castile in a St. Paul, Minnesota suburb. Three cities, three deaths, three instances where police officers were on the hot seat for killing Blacks. There would be no federal action in the cases and in one case, the slaying of Sterling, there were no state charges and in the other two cases of Gray and Castillo, there was a quick acquittal.

The odds, though, were always long that Rice, just like the three other Baltimore officers who were acquitted in the Gray case, and the officers involved in the slaying of Sterling and Castile, wouldn't have to worry about a conviction or indictment. Here's why. The victims, Gray, Sterling and Castile, as in a disproportionate number of other cases of police slayings, were young African-Americans or Hispanics.

*   *   *   *   *

It has always been an uphill battle for prosecutors to overcome pro-police attitudes and an even steeper uphill battle to overcome negative racial stereotypes. Stanford University researchers in 2014 found that even when many whites are presented with evidence that the criminal justice system is loaded with racial bias toward blacks they are more likely to support tough, draconian laws such as three strikes, tough sentencing and increased incarceration. The galling conclusion of the researchers was that informing many whites that African-Americans are significantly over-represented in the prison population "may actually bolster support for the very policies that perpetuate the inequality." The names of the countless Black victims stand as an indictment of the nation's refusal to admit that crime, violence, terrorism, and dysfunctionality can come with faces of all colors, genders, and classes and income levels.

How to change that and more?

The National Black MBA Association, New York, in 2011 recognized the chilling fact that America's congenital racial typecasting of Blacks has inflicted, and continues to inflict, a horrific toll on how minorities and especially African-Americans are viewed and treated from the streets to the courts to the prisons to the schools to the workplace to the corporate boardrooms to the political and sports arenas in American society. The ingrained negative images and typecasting have had agonizing consequences in every aspect of public policy and public attitudes. The association developed an innovative program to confront the stereotyping head-on within the schools and among young persons. It warned that stereotypes are propagated deliberately, carelessly, unwittingly and continually reinforced through the media, in workplaces, and schools, by elected officials, and through business and government agencies, and most importantly, in day to day conversations and interactions. This was a great start. Here's the add-on, though, that individuals and groups can do:

• Challenge racial stereotypes with honest, if painful and uncomfortable questions. The goal is to further understanding how stereotypes color public policy, personal attitudes and practices.

• Provide balanced, positive images and examples in the media, school curriculum, and conversations of African-Americans, Hispanics, Asians, and Women as achievers, innovators, and holders of influential positions in society in politics, education, business, the arts, and the trades.

• Support efforts to remove statues and monuments in, and at, public schools and public buildings that memorialize Confederate generals and politicians and other individuals, and actions. And the companion campaigns to educate why they perpetuate racial stereotypes and divisions of African-Americans, native Americans, Hispanics, and other minorities

• Proactively use social media to expose and counter racially derogatory cracks, digs, and attacks by individuals or groups in businesses, on campuses, and in the workplace.

- Support organizations, individuals, and elected officials that are fighting to change racial disparities in the imposition of the death penalty, parole and probation, drug sentencing laws, school suspensions and expulsions and other harsh discipline measures that unfairly target African-Americans.

- Support campaigns for a living wage, and greater family support measures for low income Black women and tougher laws to prosecute rape and sexual victimization.

- Challenge police officials to strengthen their department's policies and procedures on the use of deadly force. Stiffen punishment of, including vigorous prosecution of, officers who overuse deadly force. Then continue to press for the stringent review and revamp of training programs and procedures that stress de-escalation, and the use of non-lethal weapons by police in encounters in poor Black neighborhoods. The training of officers must be continuous and imbed non-stereotypical training materials and role-playing sessions in the training of police officers regarding Blacks and minorities

- Continually promote understanding that racist stereotypes draw their life in law and public policy from the daily reinforcement by those who have power to act on their belief in those stereotypes be it Media executives, politicians, business leaders, educators, judges, and prosecutors. They must be challenged to recognize the harm and detriment that perpetuating stereotypes in American society wreaks.

One example that combined all the tactics and

approaches that can be used to change racial attitudes was the swift response to the arrest of two Black men at a Starbucks in Philadelphia in April 2018. He men were cuffed for loitering and trespass. The loud scream was that this was racial profiling. The video of their arrest went viral. There were protests, and sit-ins at the Starbucks. The manager was released. The CEO of Starbucks profusely apologized and promised on national TV shows to make changes in staff training to ensure there was no repeat of that anywhere at a Starbucks. The action around the incident was peaceful, non-violent, proactive, called attention to racial profiling, and got results.

• Promote the continued major political focus in the Trump era in blunting and beating back the worst initiatives from draconian budget cuts, the hack away at voting rights, the wild expansion of police power, gutting public education for school choice, and a benign neglect of civil rights protections. The greatest issue that has done more to feed negative racial stereotypes about young Black males and females is joblessness. Their impoverishment has made them prime targets for the courts, prison cells, police bullets, media and political vilification. The fight must be to do more, spend more, and create more job and skills training programs.

Racial stereotypes get power and resiliency from another source that can't be ignored: individuals. If a person believes that African-Americans are inherent criminals or charity cases, then that affects how they view them and treat them. In short, they become a racial stereotype. The huge challenge then is for individuals to interact, learn from, embrace, and revel in America's diverse cultures, and lifestyles. Gender, and racial differences are a nation's strength and a treasure. When that becomes an accepted reality, the fear, and hostility, and contempt that confined African-Americans to the outer margins of American society will end. The proposals to combat deep-seated racial stereotypes and fears are modest and much needed. However, they can do much to ensure that Black lives do matter.

Notes

INTRODUCTION

www.newsweek.com/donald-trump-welfare-black-white-780252

www.news.com.au/entertainment/tv/did-brian-williams-lie-about-his-hurricane-katrina-experience-too/news-story/eae31042485047ea62b0cf32d060de4a

www.nytimes.com/2018/04/15/us/starbucks-philadelphia-black-men-arrest.html

Earl Ofari Hutchinson, *The Assassination of the Black Male Image* (New York: Simon & Schuster, 1995)

http://fox8.com/2018/04/27/waffle-house-shooting-hero-james-shaw-jr-raises-165000-for-victims/

www.yahoo.com/news/many-americans-more-common-white-213528132.html

http://diverseeducation.com/article/2709/

http://news.psu.edu/story/159388/2011/03/28/research/

demographics-cloud-optimism-black-violent-crime-decrease

Chapter 1

www.latimes.com/sports/la-sp-colin-kaepernick-award-20180421-story.html

http://journalism.missouri.edu/2015/06/black-athletes-stereotyped-negatively-in-media-compared-to-white-athletes/

http://thyblackman.com/2011/03/04/athletes-who-give-their-money-away/

http://atlantablackstar.com/2018/01/31/colin-kaepernick-completes-10for10-challenge-thanks-celebrity-friends/

www.espn.com/nba/story/_/id/9863416/chris-paul-how-athletes-give-back

http://prosgiveback.com/athletes-helping-athletes/

www.espn.com/nfl/news/story?id=2743548

www.nydailynews.com/sports/football/jim-brown-applauds-athletes-protesting-article-1.2043610

www.espn.com/classic/biography/s/Ashe_Arthur.html

Chapter 2

www.huffingtonpost.com/earl-ofari-hutchinson/toms-coon-and-mammy-home-_b_47322.html

www.govtech.com/policy-management/EBay-Urged-to-Drop-Racist-Collectibles.html

www.motherjones.com/media/2016/02/david-pilgrim-understanding-jim-crow-racist-collectibles/

http://nmaahc.si.edu/blog-post/blackface-birth-american-stereotype

Rayford W. Logan, *The Betrayal of The Negro: From Rutherford B. Hayes To Woodrow Wilson* (New York: DaCapo Press, 1997)

http://time.com/3699084/100-years-birth-of-a-nation/

http://en.wikipedia.org/wiki/Racism_in_early_American_film

http://en.wikipedia.org/wiki/Stereotypes_of_African_Americans

www.complex.com/life/2018/03/national-geographic-acknowledges-decades-of-racist-coverage-white-american-point-of-view

www.ajc.com/news/national/least-109-schools-named-after-confederate-figures-study-says/U5FSI1QjlYdgZVNwh-N2XKP/

www.huffingtonpost.com/entry/trump-notwithstanding-how-we-took-lee-down_us_599615f6e4b033e0fbdec28c

www.nydailynews.com/news/crime/racism-played-role-elliot-rodger-murder-spree-experts-article-1.1806390

www.yahoo.com/news/ap-poll-majority-harbor-prejudice-against-blacks-073551680—election.html

CHAPTER 3

www.theatlantic.com/entertainment/archive/2009/01/cosby-on-meet-the-press/6565/

http://mybrownbaby.com/2013/12/black-teen-pregnancy-rates-drop-by-51-percent-thanks-to-responsible-teens/

www.cjcj.org/news/6523

http://fivethirtyeight.com/features/black-and-hispanic-students-are-making-meaningful-gains-but-its-hard-to-tell/

www.cnn.com/2015/10/16/entertainment/bill-cosby-ebony-shattered-cover-feat/index.html

http://clutchmagonline.com/2013/02/obama-goes-after-black-fathers-again/

www.pschousing.org/news/unemployment-affects-long-term-stability-families

http://articles.baltimoresun.com/1997-10-17/news/1997290022_1_merriam-webster-collegiate-dictionary-dictionary-defines-definition

Robert DeCoy, *The Nigger Bible* (Holloway House: Los Angeles, 2002)

Dick Gregory, *Nigger* (Pocket Books: New York, 1990)

http://treepony.com/analysis-of-richard-wrights-the-ethics-of-living-jim-crow/

www.nytimes.com/1993/01/24/nyregion/rap-s-embrace-of-nigger-fires-bitter-debate.html

http://magazinehistory.blogspot.com/2009/02/racism-in-american-magazines.html

http://yeyeolade.wordpress.com/2007/04/27/black-is-beautiful/

CHAPTER 4

www.cnn.com/2015/05/18/us/texas-biker-gang-brawl-shooting/index.html

www.cnn.com/2015/05/18/opinions/kohn-biker-shooting-waco/index.html

www.al.com/opinion/index.ssf/2018/03/

no_america_the_face_of_domesti.html

www.theguardian.com/commentisfree/2018/mar/23/ mark-anthony-conditt-terrorism-christianity

www.nbcnews.com/news/us-news/why-police-aren-t-calling-austin-bombing-suspect-mark-anthony-n859116

http://abcnews.go.com/US/death-stephon-clark-police-shooting/story?id=54039443

www.cnn.com/2017/10/02/politics/las-vegas-domestic-terrorism/index.html

www.cnn.com/2017/08/11/us/charlottesville-white-nationalists-rally-why/index.html

http://reverbpress.com/politics/battlegrounds/terrorism-media-robert-lewis-dear/

www.justsecurity.org/25071/reason-dylann-roof-charged-terrorism/

http://journalisms.theroot.com/why-the-las-vegas-shooter-isn-t-called-a-terrorist-1819110137

www.pri.org/stories/2015-07-21/how-do-we-define-domestic-terrorism-legal-meaning-loaded-term

Chapter 5

www.huffingtonpost.com/sophia-a-nelson/race-stereotypes-the-tray_b_3628327.html

www.cnn.com/2012/03/24/opinion/roland-martin-stereotypes/index.html

www.huffingtonpost.com/leland-ware/michael-brown-stereotypes_b_5685712.html

www.independent.co.uk/voices/comment/the-shooting-of-michael-brown-proves-once-again-how-racial-stereotyping-can-lead-to-murder-9674305.html

www.vox.com/2014/11/24/7175967/darren-wilson-charges-michael-brown-ferguson

www.huffingtonpost.com/earl-ofari-hutchinson/post_10041_b_8073492.html

CHAPTER 6

www.baltimoresun.com/news/maryland/bs-md-rally-for-richard-20170528-story.html

www.slate.com/blogs/the_slatest/2017/05/22/richard_collins_iii_murder_being_investigated_as_hate_crime.html

www.vibe.com/2017/11/white-teen-gang-related-murder-out-on-bail/

www.bostonglobe.com/metro/2015/09/29/black-defendants-more-likely-held-before-trial-than-whites-some-counties-study-finds/BP2z3aZYHkvUhy5NNxHaxL/story.html

www.cbsnews.com/news/parkland-school-shooter-nikolas-cruz-getting-fan-mail/

http://downtrend.com/71superb/new-fbi-stats-blacks-more-likely-to-commit-hate-crimes-than-any-other-race/

http://thinkprogress.org/fraternities-were-built-on-racism-so-why-are-we-surprised-when-they-do-racist-things-70db8f20aeec/

http://college.usatoday.com/2015/03/15/timeline-list-of-recent-sorority-and-fraternity-racist-incidents/

CHAPTER 7

www2.ed.gov/about/offices/list/ocr/docs/crdc-discipline-snapshot.pdf

www.sciencedirect.com/science/article/pii/S0022103115000992

www.cnn.com/2017/03/24/us/missing-black-girls-washington-dc/index.html

www.nytimes.com/2012/03/06/education/black-students-face-more-harsh-discipline-data-shows.html

www.dallasnews.com/news/news/2016/03/17/black-disabled-students-more-likely-to-be-suspended-at-charter-schools-national-study-finds

www.law.upenn.edu/live/news/2170-new-study-by-professor-david-s-abrams-confirms#.V1rX_BSxmeg

www.psychologicalscience.org/news/releases/teachers-more-likely-to-label-black-students-as-troublemakers.html

www.gunlaws.com/Gun_Free_School_Zones_Act.pdf

www.edweek.org/ew/articles/2017/01/25/black-students-more-likely-to-be-arrested.html

www.chicagotribune.com/news/ct-met-unequal-school-discipline-20120926-story.html

www.nytimes.com/2014/01/09/us/us-criticizes-zero-tolerance-policies-in-schools.html

http://news.vice.com/en_us/article/mbx9p8/betsy-devos-wants-to-end-program-designed-to-reduce-racial-bias-in-school-discipline

www.dallasnews.com/news/education/2018/04/05/

black-students-still-disciplined-often-harshly-white-peers-report-says

www.washingtonpost.com/blogs/govbeat/wp/2014/09/16/school-police-across-the-country-receive-excess-military-weapons-and-gear/

www.usatoday.com/story/opinion/2018/02/19/parkland-school-shootings-not-new-normal-despite-statistics-stretching-truth-fox-column/349380002/

www.theguardian.com/world/2014/sep/18/us-school-districts-given-free-machine-guns-and-grenade-launchers

CHAPTER 8

www.bloomberg.com/news/articles/2018-03-27/urgent-the-latest-no-charges-in-alton-sterling-s-fatal-shooting

www.thenation.com/article/why-its-impossible-indict-cop/

www.pbs.org/newshour/show/deadly-police-shootings-end-police-convictions

www.cnn.com/2017/05/18/us/police-involved-shooting-cases/index.html

www.courts.ca.gov/documents/culture_handout6.pdf

www.psychologytoday.com/us/blog/ulterior-motives/201607/juries-lawyers-and-race-bias

www.huffingtonpost.com/entry/another-cop-trial-but-will-there-be-a-conviction-this_us_590f2cd6e4b0f711807245a9

www.latimes.com/politics/la-pol-ca-new-police-transparency-legislation-20180330-story.html

CHAPTER 9

www.cnn.com/2017/03/24/us/missing-black-girls-washington-dc/index.html

http://journalismcenter.org/when-a-child-dies/missing-white-girl.html

www.denverpost.com/2013/02/14/why-do-we-seldom-hear-about-missing-black-children/

www.huffingtonpost.com/earl-ofari-hutchinson/when-a-serial-killer-targ_b_185175.html

www.stltoday.com/news/local/crime-and-courts/from-the-archives-st-louis-serial-killer-victims-were-less/article_6d10868c-b3ef-5e32-81ab-bd450eb85268.html

www.thetrace.org/2016/12/black-women-more-likely-fatally-shot-by-man-than-white-women/

www.forbes.com/sites/shenegotiates/2012/04/25/black-women-sexual-assault-and-the-art-of-resistance/#4652ee497469

http://articles.chicagotribune.com/2000-04-10/news/0004100103_1_strip-searches-intensive-searches-white-women

http://atlantablackstar.com/2016/04/01/behind-bars-6-things-you-should-know-about-black-women-in-prison/

www.npr.org/sections/codeswitch/2015/02/13/384005652/study-black-girls-are-being-pushed-out-of-school

www.washingtonpost.com/news/wonk/wp/2015/01/30/black-teens-who-commit-a-few-crimes-go-to-jail-as-often-as-white-teens-who-commit-dozens/

Donna Ann-Smith Mitchell, *Time on the Inside: Behind the Walls in a Maximum Security Women's Prison, from an Insider's View* (FMA Publishing: Los Angeles, 2006)

www.themarshallproject.org/2017/10/10/what-is-prison-like-for-women-and-girls

Chapter 10

Barack Obama, *The Audacity of Hope: Thoughts on Reclaiming the American Dream* (Vintage: New York, 2008)

http://newsone.com/194731/rangel-says-obama-needs-to-be-careful-when-he-visits-harlem/

http://thehill.com/homenews/news/215627-holder-tells-ferguson-students-he-was-a-victim-of-racial-profiling

www.theroot.com/photos/2013/08/racial_profiling_black_celebs_who_dealt_with_it.html

http://people.com/sports/former-tennis-pro-james-blake-mistakenly-arrested-by-nypd/

www.usatoday.com/story/sports/nfl/2013/11/29/racial-profiling-nfl/3779489/

www.cnn.com/2014/01/21/us/richard-sherman-response/index.html

www.usatoday.com/story/sports/nfl/columnist/bell/2017/10/16/nfl-likely-blackballed-colin-kaepernick-but-can-he-prove-collusion-evidence/770013001/

http://ew.com/article/2010/01/04/tiger-woods-vanity-fair-cover-intense-or-intimidating/

CHAPTER 11

www.salon.com/2016/05/13/bill_clinton_continues_to_defend_1994_crime_bill_that_fueled_racist_mass_incarceration/

www.cnn.com/2016/02/16/politics/hillary-clinton-civil-rights-groups-leaders-harlem/index.html

www.politifact.com/truth-o-meter/statements/2016/aug/28/reince-priebus/did-hillary-clinton-call-african-american-youth-su/

http://thehill.com/blogs/blog-briefing-room/news/241247-bill-clinton-renounces-his-1994-crime-bill

www.reuters.com/article/us-usa-election-clinton/bill-clinton-says-tough-90s-crime-bill-went-too-far-idUSKBN-0NR23G20150506

www.theatlantic.com/politics/archive/2015/05/the-tragic-politics-of-crime/392114/

www.nytimes.com/2016/04/13/opinion/did-blacks-really-endorse-the-1994-crime-bill.html

CHAPTER 12

www.cnn.com/2017/08/10/health/trump-opioid-emergency-declaration-bn/index.html

www.addictshelpline.com/opioid-vs-crack-addiction/

http://projects.publicsource.org/pittsburgh-opioid-epidemic/in-the-hypocrisy-of-the-opioid-epidemic-white-means-victim-black-means-addict.html

www.nytimes.com/2017/05/09/us/politics/jeff-sessions-sentencing-criminal-justice.html

www.cnn.com/2016/03/23/politics/john-ehrlichman-richard-nixon-drug-war-blacks-hippie/index.html

www.bostonglobe.com/opinion/editorials/2018/01/05/jeff-sessions-reignites-drug-war/eyS2EbwPRjSQ8JIoi93jnK/story.html

www.nolo.com/legal-updates/u-s-attorney-general-re-ignites-the-war-on-drugs-orders-prosecutors-to-seek-stiffer-penalties.html

CHAPTER 13

www.usatoday.com/story/life/music/2017/11/06/meek-mill-gets-prison-sentence-probation-violation-earlier-gun-and-drug-case/838448001/

www.latimes.com/sports/sportsnow/la-sp-robert-kraft-meek-mill-20180411-story.html

www.sentencingproject.org/wp-content/uploads/2016/01/Reducing-Racial-Disparity-in-the-Criminal-Justice-System-A-Manual-for-Practitioners-and-Policymakers.pdf

www.nytimes.com/2018/02/11/opinion/problem-parole.html

www.epi.org/publication/webfeatures_snapshots_archive_09172003/

http://thesocietypages.org/socimages/2015/04/03/race-criminal-background-and-employment/

http://thecrimereport.s3.amazonaws.com/2/fb/e/2362/criminal_stigma_race_crime_and_unemployment.pdf

www.chicagotribune.com/ct-youth-unemployment-urban-league-0126-biz-20160124-story.html

CHAPTER 14

www.nydailynews.com/news/national/tennessee-ceo-walt-baker-humor-e-mail-gag-comparing-michelle-obama-tarzan-chimp-article-1.176291

www.commonsensemedia.org/blog/watch-out-classic-movies-with-racial-stereotypes

www.huffingtonpost.com/2009/02/18/new-york-post-chimp-carto_n_167841.html

http://amsterdamnews.com/news/2011/apr/12/shocking-blacks-and-apes-study/

www.apa.org/pubs/journals/releases/psp-a0035663.pdf

http://eewmagazine.com/marilyn-davenport-email-calls-obama-family-monkeys.html

www.dailymail.co.uk/news/article-1378380/Official-apologizes-Obama-chimpanzee-email-Tea-party-member-fired.html

www.dailymail.co.uk/news/article-1377305/Obama-addresses-birther-issue-directly-whirlwind-day-Chicago-fundraising.html

www.huffingtonpost.com/earl-ofari-hutchinson/the-vile-fascination-with_b_494985.html

http://news.stanford.edu/pr/2008/pr-eber-021308.html

CHAPTER 15

http://thinkprogress.org/the-officers-who-killed-alton-sterling-and-philando-castile-may-not-be-punished-heres-why-e064766e3ba2/

http://newsone.com/3786135/police-convictions-killing-unarmed-black-men/

www.nytimes.com/2018/03/28/us/sacramento-stephon-clark.html

http://news.gallup.com/poll/175088/gallup-review-black-white-attitudes-toward-police.aspx

www.nydailynews.com/news/national/jurors-rodney-king-tape-article-1.2201822

http://abcnews.go.com/Entertainment/fall-rodney-king-juror-words/story?id=46712060

www.usatoday.com/story/opinion/policing/2017/12/14/jury-selection-race-policing-usa-discrimination/706549001/

Chapter 16

www.nbcnews.com/id/26803840/ns/politics-decision_08/t/poll-racial-views-steer-some-away-obama/#.WtEs0oz-buyI

http://news.newamericamedia.org/news/view_article.html?article_id=b691143fa84b3bd97da9fb684ddbcc9a

www.vox.com/identities/2017/12/15/16781222/trump-racism-economic-anxiety-study

Conclusion

http://hubpages.com/entertainment/The-Movie-Crash-and-its-many-stereotypes

http://content.time.com/time/health/article/0,8599,1870408,00.html

www.slate.com/articles/health_and_science/science/

2014/08/racial_bias_in_criminal_justice_whites_don_t_
want_to_reform_laws_that_harm.html

www.nyblackmba.org/docs/nbmbaa_CASH/nbmbaa_
CASH_2012/session_3/Overcoming%20Stereotypes.pdf

www.usatoday.com/story/money/2018/04/16/star-
bucks-promises-staff-training-after-racial-profiling-inci-
dent/520201002/

Bibliography

Michelle Alexander, *The New Jim Crow: Mass Incarceration in the Age of Colorblindness* (New York: New Press, 2012)

Jeff Benedict, *Tiger Woods* (New York: Simon & Schuster, 2018)

Michael Bennett, *Things That Make White People Uncomfortable* (Chicago: Haymarket Books, 2018)

James Blake and Carol Taylor, *Ways of Grace: Stories of Activism, and How Sports Can Bring Us Together* (New York: Amistad, 2017)

Donald Bogle, *Toms, Coons, Mulattoes, and Mammies, and Bucks: An Interpretive History of Blacks in American Films* (New York: Continuum, 2001)

Kevin Borgeson, *Terrorism in America* (Burlington, Mass.: Jones & Bartlett Learning, 2008)

John L. Burris, *Blue vs. Black: Let's End the Conflict Between Cops and Minorities* (New York: St. Martins Griffin, 2000)

Bill Cosby, *Come on, People: On the Path from Victims to Victors* (New York: Nelson, 2007)

Dominique DuBois Gilliard, *Rethinking Incarceration: Advocating for Justice That Restores* (New York: IVP Books, 2018)

David Gillbourn, *Racism and Education: Coincidence or Conspiracy?* (New York: Routledge, 2008)

Gertrude Schaffner Goldberg, *The Feminization of Poverty: Only in America?* (New York: Praeger, 1990)

Kevin Alexander Gray, *Killing Trayvons: An Anthology of American Violence* (New York: Counterpunch: 2014)

Angela J. Hattery, *African American Families Today: Myths and Realities* (New York: Rowman & Littlefield Publishers, 2015)

John Hechinger, *True Gentlemen: The Broken Pledge of Americas Fraternities* (New York: Public Affairs, 2017)

Nancy A, Heitzeg, *The School-to-Prison Pipeline: Education, Discipline, and Racialized Double Standards* (New York: Praeger, 2016)

Earl Ofari Hutchinson, *Why It's So hard to Prosecute Cops* (Los Angeles: Hutchinson eBooks, 2015)

Gwen Ifill, *The Breakthrough: Politics and Race in the Age of Obama* (New York: Doubleday, 2009)

Ibram X. Kendi, *Stamped from the Beginning: The Definitive History of Racist Ideas in America* (New York: Nation Books, 2017)

Randall Kennedy, *Nigger: The Strange Career of a Troublesome Word* (New York: Vintage, 2003)

Randall Kennedy, *Race, Crime, and the Law* (New York: Vintage, 1998)

Wesley Lowery, *They Can't Kill Us All: Ferguson, Baltimore, and a New Era in America's Racial Justice Movement* (New York: Little Brown & Company, 2016)

Haki R, Madhubti, *Taking Bullets: Terrorism and Black Life in Twenty-first Century America Confronting White Nationalism, Supremacy, Privilege, Plutocracy and Oligarchy* (Chicago: Third World Press, 2016)

Doris Marie Provine, *Unequal under Law: Race in the War on Drugs* (Chicago: University of Chicago Press, 2007)

Doug McAdams and Karin Kloss, *Deeply Divided: Racial Politics and Social Movements in Postwar America* (New York: Oxford University Press, 2014)

Jody Miller, *Getting Played: African American Girls, Urban Inequality, and Gendered Violence* (New York: NYU Press, 2008)

Monique W. Morris, *Pushout: The Criminalization of Black Girls in Schools* (New York: The New Press, 2016)

Barack Obama, *The Audacity of Hope: Thoughts on Reclaiming the American Dream* (New York: Crown Books, 2006)

Mark Peffley, *Justice in America: The Separate Realities of Blacks and Whites* (New York: Cambridge University Press, 2010)

Leonard Pitts, *Racism in America: Cultural Codes and Color Lines in the 21st Century* (New York: Herald Books, 2016)

Charlotte Pierce-Baker, *Surviving the Silence: Black Women's Stories of Rape* (New York: W.W. Norton, 2000)

Beth E. Richie, *Arrested Justice: Black Women, Violence, and America's Prison Nation* (New York: Nation Books, 2010)

William C. Rhoden, *Forty Million Dollar Slaves: The Rise, Fall, and Redemption of the Black Athlete* (New York: Broadway Books, 2007)

Richard Rothstein, *The Color of Law: A Forgotten History of How Our Government Segregated America* (New York: Liveright, 2018)

Thomas M. Shapiro, *The Hidden Cost of Being African American: How Wealth Perpetuates Inequality* (New York: Oxford University Press, 2005)

Carol M. Swain, *The New White Nationalism in America: Its Challenge to Integration* (New York: Cambridge University, 2004)

Richard Thomas, *Drug Conspiracy: We Only Want the Blacks* (New York: New South Books, 2011)

Charles V. Willie and Richard J. Reddick, *A New Look at Black Families 6th Edition* (New York: Rowman & Littlefield Publishers, 2010)

Keeanga-Yamahtta Taylor, *From #BlackLivesMatter to Black Liberation* (Chicago: Haymarket Books, 2016)

Gary Younge, *Another Day in the Death of America: A Chronicle of Ten Short Lives* (New York: Nation Books, 2016)

David Zirin, *What's My Name, Fool? Sports and Resistance in the United States* (Chicago: Haymarket Books, 2005)

Index

About the Author

Earl Ofari Hutchinson is an author of multiple books on race and politics in America. His latest books are How Obama Won and *50 Years Later: Why the Murder of Dr. King Still Hurts* (Middle Passage Press). He is a frequent commentator on *RT America* news and past commentator on MSNBC and CNN. He is a weekly co-host of the *Al Sharpton Show* on Radio One. He is the host of the weekly *Hutchinson Report* on KPFK 90.7 FM Los Angeles and the Pacifica Network.

CPSIA information can be obtained
at www.ICGtesting.com
Printed in the USA
FSHW01n0420130618
49124FS